BUILDING BLK WEALTH

Avoid The Financial Sins Of The Past That Cause Struggle, Trauma & Pain

---

Benjamin Green

Certified Financial Fiduciary &
Wealth Preservationist

Quick Summary of Disclaimer & Disclosures:
This book provides general information. You should seek professional advice from expert professionals if attempting to implement any of the strategies in this book. Therefore, the author, the company, and the publisher disclaim any responsibility for liability, loss or risk incurred as a direct or indirect consequence of the application of any research in this book.

Full Disclaimer & Disclosures:
This book is meant to provide general information on financial subjects. It is not meant to be the reader's only source of information on complex financial subjects. Readers are instructed to seek professional advice from competent professionals on any of the topics discussed in this book. This book contains ideas, facts, and opinions of the author and/or the publisher, and is distributed with the understanding that the information in this book is current only at the time of at which it was written. While every effort has been made to ensure that the information is accurate, mistakes in content and presentation may have occurred. Therefore, the author, the company, and the publisher disclaim any responsibility for liability, loss or risk incurred as a direct or indirect consequence of the application of any research in this book.

The author and Ready2Retire™ makes no representations or warranties about the accuracy, reliability, completeness or timeliness of the content and does not recommend or endorse any specific information herein. Investment products, annuity products, and life insurance products involves risk including the potential loss of principal. No investment strategy can guarantee a profit or protect against loss in periods of declining values. Opinions expressed as written or recorded are subject to change at any time without notice and are not intended to be used as investment advice or to predict future performance. Past performance does not guarantee future results. Consult your financial professional before making any investment decision. This information is designed to provide general information on the subjects covered.

"Nothing in this world can take the place of persistence. Talent will not: nothing is more common than unsuccessful men with talent. Genius will not; unrewarded genius is almost a proverb. Education will not: the world is full of educated derelicts. Persistence and determination alone are omnipotent."

Calvin Coolidge

What are the true keys to building & preserving wealth?

Here are the keys in summary:

1. Education (learning from books/websites/videos/successful people & advisors)
2. Emulation (learning from others and not re-inventing the wheel)
3. Implementation (Action)
4. Persistence
5. Focus
6. Iteration (Kaizen (改善) -> Constant Education & Improvement)

That's it. If you follow these 6 keys, you will be successful over time.

The Truth - Part I

I wrote Building BLK Wealth™ to cover everything when it comes to building & preserving generational wealth.

What do I mean by "everything"? I mean EVERYTHING! This book is comprehensive… It's 43 chapters… And over 280 pages.

If you are a regular person who doesn't want to read through all of this, that's not a problem. Just book a time with one of our team members at: https://www.ready2retire.net/schedule-consult and we'll create a customized wealth building & preservation strategy that is relevant for your particular situation.

The Truth - Part II

The book Building BLK Wealth™ was written to help everyone and anyone that wants to build wealth and improve their lives. Although this book draws specific attention to the unbelievably alarming potential plight of Black Americans, the contents of this book can be utilized by all Americans. America is stronger when everyone has opportunities to build wealth. In the book Building BLK Wealth, "BLK" symbolizes:

a. Building Lifelong Knowledge
b. Building Lifelong Kapital (the German word for capital)
c. Boldly Leveraging Knowledge
d. Business, Legacy, Knowledge
e. Building Lifelong K's (thousands)
f. Better Lives & Knowledge

No matter the meaning that you choose when you read the book, we hope that you use this book to help you build wealth, health, and happiness.

The Truth - Part III

This book should contain very little that people find "controversial". Because its "actionable". Black Americans don't have time to mess around with political "correctness", since by some measures, Black wealth may go to ZERO by the year 2053, so this book is designed to be neither "politically correct" nor "politically incorrect". This book was written to help people get things done. This book is designed to help you:

- Build wealth
- Protect wealth
- Enjoy greater financial, mental, and physical health
- Improve the lot of your family and all Americans by educating one segment that has fallen behind economically.

With that said, let's get to work.

TABLE OF CONTENTS

FOREWORD

By: Alan Grissom
CEO of 12 South Capital
Creator of the S&P 500 IQ Index
Former Head of Business, North America - S&P Dow Jones Indices

The journey to understanding wealth—what it truly means, how to cultivate it, and how to preserve it —has long been a path littered with myths, distractions, and systemic challenges for millions of Americans of all types. Ben's "Building BLK Wealth" serves as a beacon of clarity and empowerment, cutting through the noise to address the urgent need for economic equity and financial literacy within the Black community and beyond.

Ben's voice is one of both authenticity and authority. He doesn't shy away from sharing his own missteps—those pivotal failures that taught him the critical lessons this book now offers to all who are willing to learn. Through his experiences, he illuminates the intersection of personal resilience and strategic action, and in doing so, he builds a case for why the stakes have never been higher.

As someone who has witnessed firsthand the transformative power of informed decision-making, intentional planning, and spurning conventional wisdom, I am inspired by Ben's commitment to arming readers with practical tools for financial growth. This book goes beyond theory, presenting actionable steps that can guide individuals and families toward building generational wealth—steps that are accessible to everyone, regardless of where they are starting from.

"Building BLK Wealth" is not just a book; it's a call to action. Ben challenges us to rethink the conventional wisdom, to embrace financial education as a lifelong pursuit, and to take ownership of our economic futures. He reminds us that wealth is not just about dollars and cents—

it's about freedom, legacy, and the ability to shape a better tomorrow for our families and communities.

As you turn these pages, be prepared to reflect, to challenge your assumptions, and most importantly, to act. Whether you are a seasoned investor or someone just beginning your financial journey, Ben's unwavering commitment to showcasing the best financial strategies for Americans, coupled with his invaluable insights, will meet you where you are and help guide you to where you want to be.

It is an honor to introduce this vital work, and I am confident that it will leave an indelible impact on its readers, as it has on me.

- Alan Grissom

INTRODUCTION

Can you feel the struggle? It's okay to say yes. Because there is a struggle going on… And it's happening right here in America.

What if I told you that it is projected that we are ONE generation away from the United States of America experiencing the level of poverty of a Third World Country?

Would you believe me?

Probably not because of the WMDs (weapons of mass distraction). But it's true. As of 2024, according to the Federal Reserve's Survey of Consumer Finances, the median net worth of Black American families was approximately $44,900. By comparison, and not by competition, the median net worth of White American families was approximately $284,500.

But did you know that in only one generation from now (by 2053), the median net worth of Black American families is projected to be ZERO ($0)? If these projections in the "Road to Zero Wealth" report by the Institute for Policy Studies are true, then this will be a seismic catastrophe for all Americans, not just Black Americans.

Can you imagine your children and grandchildren experiencing the level of poverty of a Third World Country? Can you imagine 10.4 million Black American families struggling even more than they struggle today? It has been said that when America has a cold, Black America has pneumonia. But, God works in mysterious ways.

What are the chances that I would meet a well-known wealth preservationist & certified financial fiduciary®, who happens to be a Black American, working on his magnum opus (the most important work of his life) one morning in the sauna?

I still remember my first encounter and introduction to Benjamin (Ben) Green. I had my eyes closed praying and meditating when I heard an assertive voice say, "you know, around the world the sauna is considered a sacred place for meditation."

He was respectfully speaking to the chatter boxes in the sauna with us. And it worked, they stopped talking so much, and I was able to go deeper in to my meditation. I was grateful.

Several minutes went by and once I opened my eyes, I realized it was just Ben and I in the sauna. I hesitated because I didn't want to break the sacred rule, but felt I had to introduce myself to him... Even though he was in deep focus. And, I'm glad I did.

Ben Green is the most brilliant financial mind I have ever encountered... And he has become a great friend of mine to boot. He cares deeply about the "Road to Zero Wealth" problem facing the future generations of Americans.

I feel blessed to have the opportunity to help him raise awareness and solve this potential seismic financial catastrophe facing all Americans, not just Black Americans. Building BLK Wealth is the most important book of this generation. I encourage you to answer the call and read this incredible book with your family and loved ones, just like I am.

God bless,

Anthony M. Ragland
CEO of BeGreat!™ Agency

CHAPTER 1

CONVENTIONAL WISDOM

On Friday, March 11, 2011 at 2:45 pm Tokyo time, I was ballin'! I had just moved back to Tokyo, the world's largest city. I was six weeks into a VP of Asia Pacific role where I was managing 10 staff members who had asked the big boss to bring me back to Japan.

I was being paid a great salary (especially for a single guy), I had a dope apartment near the train station in Tokyo's equivalent of Beverly Hills, and my "Pimp Pad" furniture was arriving the next day to top everything off. I recall it vividly. It was around 2:45 pm and I was:

A. Going over final revenue projections for Q3 with Yuko, my Japanese country manager
B. Thinking about the massive bonus I was about to receive after we hit our numbers in Q3
C. Congratulating myself on the furniture that was about to arrive at my Pimp Pad
D. Smiling inside because of the 3 dates I had set up over the long holiday weekend starting in just 3 hours (I did mention that I was single, right?)
E. Admiring Tokyo Tower from the top floor of our office
D. Reflecting on how far I had come from the country roads of South Carolina and the streets of Atlanta

To put it mildly, I was pretty pleased with myself… I thought I was on top of the world at 2:45 pm Tokyo time.

And then – SNAP.

Or… "Rumble" to be exact.

On Friday, March 11, 2011 at 2:46 pm, my world changed forever.

One hundred miles up and a few miles off the coast of Japan near a city called Fukushima, the Earth started shaking in what became one of the largest earthquakes in human history.

In 20 seconds, my staff and I went from confusion & silence, to concern, to panic, and then to hauling ass down the steps and outside of the 9-story building that I thought was going to collapse and kill us all.

I've experienced earthquakes before, so I thought this one was going to be like the other ones. The previous seven earthquakes I had been through weren't a big deal at all. A little rumbling, and they were gone in a few seconds.

On March 9th (two days before this one) we had a 7.4 magnitude earthquake that lasted about 10 seconds. It shook us up a good bit, but we shook it off and headed out for a team lunch right after it.

For the earthquake-uninitiated (which I pray to God you are), the amount of energy released during an earthquake increases by a factor of about 32 for every level you go up.

For example, a magnitude 6.0 earthquake releases 32 times more energy than a magnitude 5.0; a 7.0 releases about 1,000 times more energy, and a magnitude 8.0 releases about 32,000 times more energy than a 5.0. The March 11th Fukushima earthquake was a 9.0.

In earthquake preparation drills, the conventional training is to "shelter where you are", or stay where you are inside the building. Why? Because many people die when coming out of buildings due to falling windows and other debris.

But in that moment, when I realized I was responsible for 10 lives, and when I realized that my parents would probably have to come retrieve my body from Tokyo, I defied conventional wisdom and called my team to action. Or in plain English, I looked at a few of my team members, saw the concern turn to fear in their eyes, and told everybody to haul ass down the 9 flights of stairs. I was the last one out as we hauled ass to safety and stable ground, thankfully without any injuries along the way.

****

Little did I know, about one hundred miles north along the coast, in a small fishing village named Fukushima, the same decision-making process was playing itself out at 2 elementary schools.

At one elementary school, the teachers followed the conventional wisdom and the earthquake training drills they had been given time and time again. They told about 80 students to gather in the courtyard just like they had practiced.

At the other school down by the beach, the Japanese teachers at that school analyzed the situation, thought about the conventional wisdom, and at the moment of truth, said "Ikimashoo!" (Let's get out of here)! Those teachers grabbed the students and literally headed for the hills.

Unfortunately & fortunately, the rest is history. The 80 children who were led by their teachers that followed the conventional wisdom were lost forever. They all perished at the snap of a finger in the tsunami that ultimately claimed 20,000 lives.

But what happened to the brave, out-of-the box thinking teachers who defied conventional wisdom? They lived, and so did the children that they were responsible for.

****

In the exact same way, with the exact same type of decision process, today millions of Americans of all backgrounds face critical periods in their lives where they have to block out the conventional wisdom, mass media, and WMDs (weapons of mass distraction) as they decide what actions to take and what path to follow to improve their lives and the lives of people they care about. The average American is broke.

- Sixty percent (60%) of Americans live paycheck to paycheck.

- Fifty percent (50%) of Americans have less than $1,000 in emergency savings in a bank account.

- Forty percent (40%) of Americans have their highest credit card debt of all time.

- But perhaps the most confusing and surprising stat, is that thirty-six percent (36%) of people who make over $250,000 a year live paycheck to paycheck.

To top it off, tens of millions of Americans have deferred their student loans, have little hope of saving up enough money to buy a house, and are delaying the start of their families due to a number of factors including debt, low savings for a home purchase, zero dollars ($0) in retirement savings, and the fact that raising a child will cost $300,000 on average going forward.

In a country that accounts for only 5% of the world's population but 25% of the world's GDP and 60% of the world's stock market capitalization, these numbers above represent a great tragedy, but an even greater opportunity.

The United States has created more wealth for its citizens than any country in history. While this book shines a light on the challenge of wealth creation and preservation for Black Americans, the mission of this book is to help hard-working, self-aware Americans (of all hues) harness these wealth generation opportunities and build better futures for themselves and their families to make this country healthier, happier, and wealthier for all.

In the coming chapters you will be able to dig into the topics that are most relevant to you as you embark on your wealth-building and wealth preservation journey.

God bless you, and I wish you godspeed on your wealth building journey.

CHAPTER 2

PERSONAL FAILURES

"There is nothing to be learned from the second kick of a mule."
– Mark Twain

"If failure is not an option, success is eventually guaranteed".
– B.G.

Everyone can tell you about their accomplishments and their wins. That's fine and dandy, but true growth often stems from lessons that only failure (or learning from others' failures) can provide. Each misstep offers lessons that, when embraced, can guide us toward greater success. Here are five personal and professional failures from my past, what I learned from them, and how they shaped my journey to building my career & wealth. The whole point of this book is to make sure that you don't "reinvent the wheel" and repeat the same mistakes.

---

1. Academic Failures

- Lost Scholarship at Morehouse College

After my sophomore year, I lost my full academic scholarship due to a lack of focus and direction. I became a college dropout, with little intention of returning, and no solid plan to move forward.

Lesson Learned: Prioritize focus and persistence. Education is a privilege, not a given.

- Debt for a Second Chance

Returning to college required taking out $28,000 in loans (equivalent to $58,000 today). Taking on debt hurt a tremendous amount, but this debt, coupled with bumping heads with a finance and economics professor who eventually became my mentor (Dr. John Handy) during the first week of my junior year, helped me to refocus and make straight A's for the rest of my time in college.

Lesson Learned: Failing doesn't mean the end. With a plan and a support system, recovery and even excellence are possible.

- Financial Mismanagement

During college, I almost lost the condo my parents purchased due to poor money management.

Lesson Learned: Financial literacy is critical, especially for young adults navigating the path to independence.

---

2. **Real Estate Missteps**

- Missed Opportunity in Brazil

Passed on a beachfront condo investment with my father for $20,000 —a decision we both regretted.

Lesson Learned: Always evaluate opportunities with a long-term perspective. Hindsight and inaction can be really expensive.

- Listened to Poor Advice

Skipped buying a condo near a university after a misinformed family member discouraged me. The property appreciated significantly while I missed out.

Lesson Learned: Diversify perspectives and seek additional counsel. Sometimes the best path is a blend of advice and intuition.

---

3. Investment Blunders

- Bitcoin Losses

I was an early investor (2013–2014) but lost money during the Mt. Gox exchange collapse in Japan. If I had been implementing DCA (dollar-cost averaging) strategies since 2014 in Bitcoin, while doing more research on ways to securely acquire and store it, this would have led to larger financial wins.

Lesson Learned: Consistent research and dollar-cost averaging (DCA) are essential to wealth-building, especially in volatile markets.

- Wrong Life Insurance Choice

Was sold a Variable Universal Life (VUL) insurance in my 20s without an explanation of the high fees and complexity of the product.

Lesson Learned: Simplicity often wins. Today, I rely on simple, cash-value whole life insurance for wealth preservation and legacy building.

4. General Missteps

- Stopped Dollar-Cost Averaging (DCA)

Used DCA early in my 20s with Sharebuilder but didn't maintain the habit after the platform's closure.

Lesson Learned: Automate savings and investments as much as possible to ensure consistency and build wealth even during periods of volatility, no matter what.

5. Entrepreneurial Failures

- Trial and Error

Inside our independent insurance brokerage Insurance Advantage, we have experimented with dozens of solutions and products that didn't fit. But we've also found over 2 dozen products, carriers, and services that fit our team's capabilities and vision just right.

Lesson Learned: "Fail fast" and learn faster. Persistence and adaptability are keys to finding your niche.

What These Failures Taught Me

Failure, though painful, is a powerful teacher. Here are the principles I've embraced:

1. Evaluate Every Opportunity: Don't dismiss chances because they seem risky or unconventional.

2. Educate Myself: Financial literacy and self-awareness are non-negotiable.

3. Seek Mentors and Diverse Perspectives: Learn from others while trusting your instincts.

4. Consistency Is Critical: Automated habits—whether in saving, learning, or action—lead to long-term success.

5. Adaptability Over Rigidity: The ability to pivot can transform setbacks into opportunities.

Failures are not final. They are stepping stones that can pave the way to success if you're resilient and seek more counsel, or just get back up, learn from your mistakes, and try again. Rarely is wealth built without stumbling blocks. What matters is how you rise and rebuild.

CHAPTER 3

THE FIVE THIEVES

With this backdrop, the split between haves and have nots is widening. And also against this backdrop, even for the haves, whatever wealth you have is under constant attack by "The Five Thieves":

The Five Thieves

Thief #1 – **Taxes** – While 50% of Americans pay no income tax, many Americans pay up to 50% of their overall income towards federal, state, municipal, property, utility, phone, cable, auto, sales, and other taxes.

Thief #2 – **Fees** – Fees is a bad 4-letter word. Most Americans get a little annoyed by the cable, phone, utility, and other usage fees they pay. And all those fees suck. But the biggest blood sucker of all can be the fees you pay by following the conventional wisdom from 1952 of holding a portfolio of stocks and bond mutual funds while shelling out 1– 2.5% a year in 401k, TSP, IRA, and other retirement account fees.

If you have a retirement account, when is the last time you looked at the fees? Mutual funds alone can include over 10 different types of fees. How about your financial advisor's fees? Are those separate, or included in that .5 – 1.5%? And how much can they cost you if you're compounding over 30 years?

Thief #3 – **Inflation** – Just for starters, Medicare Part B, whose monthly price is set by the U.S. federal government, was $15.50 in 1985. In 2025 it will be $185. Simple math says that's 12x (12 times the price from 40 years ago). Has your salary gone up 12x in the last 2 decades? If you're beginning your career, do you have the opportunity to 12x your earnings in 2-3 decades? What are you going to do to beat that type of inflation?

Thief #4 – **Volatility & Inconsistent Returns** – Imagine building your wealth like constructing a skyscraper, brick by brick. Now picture a hurricane knocking loose some of those bricks every year. This is what volatility and inconsistent returns do to your wealth-building efforts and your peace of mind.

When you're still working and contributing to your portfolio, you may be able to recover from these market swings. However, once you stop working and start relying on your life savings to fund your income in retirement, the stakes change dramatically. A big market loss early in retirement can cripple your long-term financial health. This is known as "sequence of returns risk." Simply put, if you experience significant losses early in retirement, you may have to sell more shares of your investments to maintain your lifestyle, which leaves fewer assets to recover when the market rebounds.

Inconsistent returns also disrupt compounding growth. For example, if you experience a 50% loss one year, you need a 100% gain just to get back to where you started. This reality makes it difficult to sustain long-term growth, and have a reliable income in retirement.

For wealth builders, reducing volatility is critical. Strategies like true diversification and asset allocation (not the 1952 version that is still sold to most Americans), hedging, and investing in products with built-in downside protection can help minimize the damage and lock in future income. For retirees, the focus shifts to income planning and risk management. Without a plan to weather volatility, you may face the risk of running out of money in retirement. Don't let this thief rob you of your financial future.

Thief #5 – **WMDs** (weapons of mass distraction) – What is your most valuable asset? That's a trick question: It's you… You are your most valuable asset.

And what is the most valuable resource for that asset? That's another trick question: It's your time… Your time is your most valuable resource.

So how much precious time do you waste looking at social media, political news shows, or even dealing with friend or family drama?

And how much of your most valuable resource do you spend feeding your brain and body opportunities to improve your life, health, career, or finances?

Don't let the thieves rob you. Fight back.

CHAPTER 4

THE ZERO WEALTH HOUR

What makes Black wealth discussions different and more critical?

Simply put, median Black American wealth has been predicted to potentially go to $0 by 2053. And no one in this country can afford for that to happen, especially given this data:

- U.S. Government debt stands at over $36 trillion (per USdebtclock.org)
- Total U.S. Government unfunded liabilities stand at over $217 Trillion (per USdebtclock.org)
- Between 8,000 – 12,000 people per day are turning 65
- Long-Term care costs currently range between $5,000 - $15,000 per month

Additionally, Black Americans deal with a variety of additional challenges to building wealth, preserving wealth, and passing wealth on to the next generation including:

- A general lack or deficit in financial literacy
- A lack of understanding of the importance of protecting checks & assets with disability insurance and life insurance
- A lack of understanding of how to use permanent life insurance to pass money tax-free on to the next generation
- The clash between the flashy/sexy and the boring
- A focus on depreciating assets vs. appreciating assets
- The all-American desire to appear to "keep up with the Joneses"
- Taking on more student loans than their White & Asian counterparts
- Getting useless degrees from dubious "universities" that seek to exploit first-generation college students & under-represented groups
- Lacking an understanding of the importance of networks and methodically building resumes

▸Lacking an understanding of the importance of constantly upgrading the 5 closest people in business connections and networking "Room"

▸Difficult names – Life is hard enough. If your name is harder, you can do something about it. Ever heard of the famous actor Issur Danielovitch Demsky. Of course you haven't. That's because he changed his name to Kirk Douglas, and changed his fortunes.

▸The Math – According to a study by the Institute for Policy Studies and Prosperity Now in 2017, Median Black Wealth is going to Zero by the year 2053 if nothing substantive changes. For those of you that think it's not possible, I have personally reviewed thousands of cases and know it is possible, even with the average Black NBA and NFL player making millions, and with the advent of NIL money flowing into the ranks of college athletics. For the median Black individual or family, net worth is going to go to ZERO without any changes.

The numbers from SSA (Social Security Administration) bear this out, even for those that should have been able to save a substantial amount during the greatest bull market run in American history:

- According to the Social Security Administration (SSA), approximately 45% of Black beneficiaries rely on Social Security for 90% or more of their retirement income.
- About 35% of Black beneficiaries rely on Social Security for their entire income in retirement.

All Americans face the 5 Thieves, and control over the 5 Thieves can have a tremendous impact on overall health and wealth. The median White American family, with a net worth of $284,500, has some cushion, but not much, to withstand these attacks and hopefully plan to grow more wealth. However, given the rise in stock, real estate, and cryptocurrency prices over the last decade, $284,500 is low.

The median Hispanic family has a net worth of $61,600, according to the Hispanic Wealth Project.

But the median Black American family has a net worth of $44,900. This means that the median Black family has 0 (ZERO) margin for error. Even the smallest financial hiccup can cause an emergency.

What Can Be Controlled

You will notice that with the exception of the current math on median wealth, which is what it is, every challenge above is something that can be controlled.

Issues with math, reading, speaking, and tech skills? We can fix that.

A lack of financial literacy? We can fix that.

A focus acquiring appreciating assets (stocks, real estate, and REITs for example) vs. depreciating assets?We can fix that.

A reduction in the number of people taking on large amounts of student loan debt to get crappy degrees that will not improve their career prospects? We can fix that.

In this book we're going to focus on:

- What we can control
- What we can improve
- What we can be taught or educated on
- What we can take sustainable, productive action on

You will specifically never see me talk about racism. We're going to focus on what we can control. Everything else can work itself out.

CHAPTER 5

WHY CARE?

WHO CARES ABOUT BLACK WEALTH?
AND WHY SHOULD YOU CARE?

But seriously, who cares? And why should anyone other than Black Americans care? Finally, what are the consequences of Black wealth going to $0 by 2053 (or earlier)?

1. A Social Security catastrophe: The US needs as many productive people contributing to the system as possible, and the number of people supporting the Social Security program is lower than ever.

2. Medicare & Medicaid fiscal catastrophe: Black wealth going to zero will cause (and already causes) a myriad of health/stress related issues); and the US and individual states can't afford more people from a percentage standpoint to go onto Medicaid; Currently Medicare & Medicaid are 27% of federal budget, and that number is growing every year as our population ages. This growing budget nightmare is a problem for everyone.

3. Demographic drop-off: It can cost over $300,000 to raise a child now, and births peaked in 2008. Now even less children will be born as people hold off on having kids until they can afford it, or will at least hold off on having multiple kids. Why is this catastrophic for everyone (White, Black, Hispanic, Asian, and everyone else) who lives in the US? Social Security and Medicare started out being supported by 16 workers to every 1 beneficiary. Now the ratio is 3 to 1. Bottom Line: WE NEED SOME MORE KIDS TO PAY FOR ALL THESE (OLDER) MORE SEASONED PEOPLE!

4. Crime: On average, how many millionaires or Harvard grads do you hear about robbing people or shooting people? When people are

poor, crime ratchets up. I've seen this firsthand in Brazil where the wealth gap is high, but the walls to keep out would-be robbers are even higher in mega cities like Sao Paulo and Rio de Janeiro.

5. A Reduction in Spending: For businesses, colleges, hospitality, all other private or public enterprises, Black American spending accounts for 10% of the economy. Imagine the impact that it would have on the economy if Black spending dropped by just 10%? How about 20 or 30%? This would decrease the US GDP by 1, 2, or 3% a year, almost certainly pulling the nation into recession more often. Imagine if colleges saw a 10 – 30% drop off in Black students because their families were too broke to send them to school? And imagine the overall drop in the economy if Black families experienced a 20 – 50% drop in median wealth?

Make no mistake about it, Black American wealth going to ZERO will negatively impact every citizen and business in the U.S.

AND WHY DO I CARE?

I care because no one in the world's most powerful country should be broke. And no family will go to ZERO wealth in 30 years if they make the adjustments today. I also care because the U.S. will be a more miserable place to live if Black Americans go to zero wealth.

SO, WHAT IS THE SOLUTION, AND CAN THE TREND BE REVERSED?

Some of the solutions are surprisingly simple, and yes, this trend can be reversed. In fact, it must be reversed.

Specifically in the Black community, where the wealth situation is critical (at an emergency situation), Black Americans must:

- Throw much of the conventional wisdom for building wealth out the door, much like the Japanese teachers who saved their students did
- Rethink everything they've ever been taught about how to build wealth (including the need to go to college)
- Re-engineer the mindset to focus on achieving excellence in:
    - A. Great habits including:
        - Making your bed every morning
        - Creating an energetic, winning morning routine
        - Eating an energy-enhancing breakfast including proteins and complex carbs or fruits/vegetables
        - Automating savings & investment
    - B. Education (but not necessarily college) including:
        - Mastering the English language (speaking, reading, writing)
    - C. Career Optimization
    - D. Financial Literacy (or receiving expert financial advice)
    - E. Longer term planning
    - F. Longer term investing
    - G. Generational wealth building
    - H. Systematically & strategically focus on removing distractions (social media, mass media, family, etc.) and focus on building health, wealth, and happiness

The purpose of Building Black Wealth is to help Black Americans do just that: Build their health, wealth, & happiness.

Building wealth goes hand in hand with enjoying freedom. Building wealth is a basic human right at its core. In fact, the ability to build wealth is more important than voting rights. Don't believe me? How many people don't vote? Up to 50% in most elections.

But how many people can afford to not build wealth? Only a few.

CHAPTER 6

STREET CRED

This is the least important part of this book. But here's my quick bio:

- 1 Amazon best seller book: "The Global Superstar™: How Your Students Can Develop An Advantage over Global Competition"
- 1 full academic scholarship: I obtained 1 full scholarship to Morehouse college which I lost after 2 years.
- 1 college dropout: I had one experience of dropping out of college (with no plan to come back).
- 1 flood: I've experienced one flood.
- 1 tsunami: I experienced one tsunami.
- 1 nuclear meltdown & explosion in Japan.
- 1 "Boyz in the Hood" event: One experience of my house getting shot up in college.
- 1 Chicken Flu: One Hong Kong chicken flu experience.
- 1 Mad Cow: One experience with Mad Cow disease in Europe.
- 1 Dengue: One bad case of Dengue Fever in Thailand.
- 1 case of Montezuma's Revenge in Macau.
- 1 case of being temporarily being "detained" in Beijing.
- 1 case of temporarily being "questioned" by police in Bangkok.
- 1 case of temporarily "losing" my younger brother in Tokyo.
- 1 instance of being "welcomed" by local cops in Boracay.
- 1 year as a tackling dummy in middle school football
- 1 "tussle" aka fight in Madrid
- 1 fight in college football (practice)
- 1 chicken factory job (day and night shift)
- 1 Chinese wheel manufacturer representative contract (for 2 years)
- 1 case of being questioned by police in Beijing
- 1 case of being questioned by police in Bangkok
- 1 introduction to a local sheriff in the Philippines

- 1 trademark filing in Japan (for First Fridays Japan)
- 1 office opened for the State of South Carolina in Japan
- 2 wonderful daughters (that are smarter than me)
- 2 night shift jobs
- 2 times working illegally in a foreign country
- 2 times being briefly "interviewed" by police in Japan
- 2 mini-books written: "How to live and work in Brazil"; "Build Generational Wealth & Happiness: The Global Superstar™ Guide to Success Post-Covid"
- 3 failed businesses
- 3 cases of being "questioned" by Japanese police in Tokyo.
- 3 Amazon best seller categories held for 3 days in 2016
- 4 years living in a trailer
- 4 fights in elementary school
- 4 successful business startups
- 4 countries (lived and worked in)
- 5 years of high school and college football
- 5 hurricanes and typhoons
- 5 states worked and lived in (SC, GA, Connecticut, Washington, Tennessee)
- 6 economic development (business recruitment agencies) consulted
- 7 languages studied (English, Spanish, Latin, Japanese, Portuguese, Italian, French)
- 10 years living overseas: 8 in Japan, 1 in Spain, & 1 in Brazil.
- 10 non-profit boards: I've served on over 10 education, university, chamber of commerce, and non-profit boards.
- 10 languages spoken in business or travel (English, Spanish, Japanese, Portuguese, Chinese, French, German, Tagalog, Thai, Korean)
- 28+ countries: I've traveled to 28 countries (from the richest to the poorest).
- 31 states visited
- 40 parties thrown: Co-founded First Fridays Tokyo, and I've thrown over 40 parties in Tokyo, Atlanta, and Osaka.
- 42 jobs: I've had 42 jobs (from overnight chicken factory worker & Big Lots overnight shelf stocker to Insurance Broker & Owner

of one of the largest independent insurance brokerages in the Southeast; Best job? Volunteer & Regional Director for the Foundation for Financial Literacy and the Foundation for Fiduciary Education. And working with my clients of course.

- 100 people placed in jobs: I've helped place over 100 people in jobs, including several overseas.
- 250+ cities: I've visited over 250 large cities.
- 1000+ towns: I've visited over 1,000 towns and villages.
- 1000+ earthquakes experienced
- 5,000 jobs: I've directly and indirectly recruited investments that created over 5,000 jobs.
- 5,000 clients: My firms have helped over 5,000 clients.
- 10,000 people educated: My firms have educated over 10,000 on health, Medicare, life, disability, long-term care, and retirement planning.
- 10,000 spoken to: I've taught and spoken to over 10,000 students, adults, teachers, administrators, and church attendees.
- $16,000: Amount I was paid to create The Strategic Plan for the State of South Carolina (before the project was canceled)
- 37,000 in student loan debt: After I finished undergrad and graduate school I had $37,000 (equivalent of $63,500 today) in student loan debt to pay off.
- 38 years old: The age that I paid my student loan debt off.
- $100,000,000 ($100 million): I'm directly responsible for recruiting over $100 million in investment to the Southeast from various states and countries.
- $2,000,000,000 ($2 billion): I'm indirectly responsible for helping to recruit over $2 billion of foreign direct investment into the Southeast to create jobs and positively change people's lives.

Summary

I'm not a politician. I'm a patriot. I'm a businessman. And I'm a concerned American citizen that sees the storm that lies ahead, not just for Black Americans, but for all Americans.

And if you're not concerned about one group's wealth going to ZERO by 2053, you might be in denial about the ramifications of this emergency for the entire country.

The consequences of failing to take HUGE action will be as severe as they were on the shores of Fukushima.

The situation calls for intensive education, effort, and most importantly, ACTION.

So, "Ikimashoo!"

Let's go.

CHAPTER 7

PROFESSIONAL CRED

In the last **24 months**, I have:

- Become certified as a Certified Financial Fiduciary
- Traveled to Spain, Portugal, Colombia, Italy, Canada, Mexico, Scotland, Germany, Belgium, Denmark, Atlanta, Charlotte, Dallas, Las Vegas, and Salt Lake City to review economic and wealth-building models, review real estate and retirement planning options for clients, receive wealth management training, and enjoy the locales
- Been re-certified to provide Medicare and Prescription Drug assistance and enrollment
- Been re-certified and recognized as a Healthcare.gov Marketplace Circle of Champions Recipient
- Been re-certified on Annuities
- Been re-certified on Long-Term Care Planning
- Met and received training from Tom Hegna, America's #1 expert on guaranteed income and immediate annuities
- Met and received training from Ed Slott, America's #1 expert on IRA & 401k Planning
- Met and received training from David McKnight, America's #1 expert on Reducing Taxes to $0 in retirement
- Met and received training from Tom Hegna, America's #1 expert on guaranteed income and annuities
- Met and received training from Van Mueller, one of America's top Life & Annuity Insurance Agents
- Studied the groundbreaking paper "Beyond the Status Quo: A Critical Assessment of Lifecycle Investment Advice" & interviewed Dr. Aizhan Anarkulova (Emory University), part of the world-leading retirement research team that wrote this paper including Dr. Scott Cederburg (University of Arizona) and Dr. Michael O'Doherty (University of Missouri)

• Had multiple, in-depth discussions with the creator of a leading retirement income solution that was nominated by Structured Products Intelligence USA as the #1 Annuity Index in the United States

• Had our insurance brokerage Insurance Advantage invited to the Top Agents retreat for BlueCross BlueShield South Carolina

• Attended numerous wealth management and financial advisor conferences including the "Heroes of Zero" and Structured Products Intelligence USA Conference

• Been recognized as a top 15 Advisor (in addition to being one of the youngest advisors, and the only Black American Advisor) in the country by a leading retirement income solutions company

• Reached the top 5 of America's #1 Virtual, Independent Advisor Network

Why is providing this information necessary? Because there are a lot of less-than-informed "advisors" out there, including people who advertise or provide "advice" on TV and radio without having the data sets and skill sets necessary to fully provide that advice.

You **must** understand who you are getting information from before you use that information or take action on that information. And you need to understand where they have gotten their information and experience from. Period.

CHAPTER 8

THE KEY QUESTIONS

Before we get to the mindset that it takes to build and keep wealth today, here are some questions for you. Think of it as a survey or quiz.

The most important question: Do you care about building wealth? About building health? About anything? And why, or why not? Lastly, what are you going to do about it?

Once you've answered this, here are some additional questions:

Focus

Do you have any goals? Do you carry them around in your back pocket? Are they written down? Do you review them regularly?

Do you care about building health or wealth? Do you care about making the lives of your family, friends, and community better?

Is the light on upstairs for you when it comes to building and preserving wealth?

Are you too busy listening to politicians, watching CNN or Fox, or watching TikTok, Facebook, or Instagram videos?

If you actually give a dang, please continue below. I'm not sure if you've ever been asked these questions.

Taxes

- Do you think federal income taxes will go up or down in the future?

- What is the current debt for the U.S. federal government? If you don't know, visit www.usdebtclock.org and prepare to be shocked.
- How much U.S. federal debt does each eligible U.S. taxpayer have "assigned" to them? If you don't know, once again, please visit www.usdebtclock.org.
- Did you know that if you have an adjusted gross income of $43,614 or more, you're in the top 50% of all taxpayers?
- Did you know that the top 50% of taxpayers pay 97.1% of all individual federal income taxes?
- Did you know that half of US citizens pay 0% federal income tax?
- What is the current debt for your state government?
- Does your state take income taxes?
- How much debt does your state have?
- How much debt does your state have per capita?
- Did you realize that the average American spends the first 15 of every 40 work hours each week working for the federal, state, and municipal governments i.e. working off the taxes?
- Did you realize the average American may work another 1-2 hours per week working to pay off fees?
- Did you realize that there are products that can allow you to grow your money tax-free or fee-free, or both tax & fee-free?

Retirement Accounts

- Do you realize that 401ks, IRAs, TSPs, 403bs, and other retirement products are financial products, not financial plans?
- Do you know who will be first and second in line for any distributions that you take from your retirement accounts (401k, TSPs, 403bs, 401(a)s)?
- Do you realize you may be 3rd or 4th in line to receive money from your 401k?
- Did you know that Wall Street and Main Street mutual funds, hedge funds, financial advisors and planners collect billions (tens or hundreds of billions?) a year in transaction and advisory fees?
- Did you know that 86% of active mutual fund managers and financial advisors don't beat the S&P 500 index over a 10-year period?

• Did you realize your traditional retirement products (401k, TSP, 403b, etc.) can be taxed up to 40% or more when you pass away?

• Did you know you may make more in retirement than you did during your career?

Financial Ruin Risk
(Not Running out of Money in Retirement)

• What chance do you have of running out of money if you have stocks, bonds, mutual funds, target date funds, or annuities?

• What do you understand about asset correlations and asymmetric returns?

• What do you understand about variable, fixed, fixed indexed, and income annuities?

• What do you understand about the differences in indexes available inside fixed indexed annuities?

• Have you read or gotten a synopsis of the Scott Cederburg papers?

Medicare/Social Security

• Do you know that peak T-65 (Baby Boomers turning 65 years old and retiring) will happen from 2022 – 2029?

• Did you realize that Social Security was based on a 16-1 worker-beneficiary ratio, and now the ratio is 3-1?

• Did you know that U.S. births peaked in 2008? (Intelligent college & university presidents do).

• Do you think Medicare premiums will rise in the next 20 years?

• Did you know that Medicare isn't "free"?

• Do you know how much Medicare premiums have risen in the last 30 years?

• Did you know that Medicare does NOT cover long-term care (nursing home or home health care) costs?

• Will Social Security be around 20 years from now?

• Do you think that the federal government will make decisions about federal debt, taxes, Social Security, Medicare, and monetary policy that don't negatively impact you in the next 20 years?

Long-Term Care (LTC)

• You know that Medicare does NOT cover long-term care costs, right?

• Did you realize that you have to technically be broke to qualify for Medicaid to cover LTC costs?

• Did you realize that the federal or state government can seize your assets to recover costs associated with providing you Medicaid for LTC coverage?

Covering Your Assets (aka Life Coverage)

• What is your greatest asset? (This is a trick question).

• What is your greatest resource for that asset?

• Do you have that asset covered at 7 – 15x its annual salary or compensation?

• Do you have permanent asset protection past a 10 or 20-year period?

• Can you think of another financial product or asset that your beneficiaries can receive tax free?

Estate Planning

• Did you know that your children can be disinherited from your will (i.e. could get $0) after you die?

• Do you have a will?

• Do you need to update your beneficiary forms for your life insurance?

• Did you realize that after you pass away, your ex will receive 100% of life insurance proceeds if you haven't updated your beneficiary forms?

- Did you realize that the beneficiaries listed on a life insurance policy will override a will?
- Do you have any trusts set up for you or your children?
- Do you realize that you don't need to be "rich" to set up a will or trust?
- Did you know that only 33% of Americans have a will set up?
- Do you know that after you pass away, your spouse can change your will?

Entrepreneurship

- Did you know that business owners can enjoy incredible tax benefits?
- Are you familiar with all of the tax write-offs that business owners can take?

Real Estate

- Do you know all the tax benefits that real estate investors can utilize to reduce their tax burdens?
- Have you ever heard of a 1035 tax exchange?
- How about a 1031 exchange???

Education

- Did you know that your children or even grad school students can go to college/university for free in other countries like Japan and Germany?
- Do you realize that your usage of 529 plans is completely controlled by the federal government?
- Do you realize there are other vehicles to save money in for your children's college funds?
- Do you think that you or your kids can be financially successful without going to college?
- Would you believe that there are 70-year olds that are still paying off student loan debt?

Career

- Are you building your resume methodically (i.e. not too many moves in too many years, increasing your positions within companies, taking on more responsibility in the company, etc.)?
- Did you pick your current location, or did it pick you?
- Are you being paid what you deserve?
- Are you taking advantage of all the company offers you?
- Are you building your network strategically and intelligently?
- What are the taxes, fees, and other costs associated with living in that city, region, or state?
- Are you in the best position?
- Are you in the best industry for your skills?
- Are you living in the best city or state (for you)?

All of these questions, if answered and thought through properly, can grow and compound your wealth over time. So please take a few moments to go through them.

CHAPTER 9

THE MINDSET

Now that you've figured out that you actually care about HEALTH, WEALTH, AND HAPPINESS, what principles does it take to build them?

1. You were made by The Creator, and you are a creator. You create your own opportunities. You create your own economy. You create your own happiness.

2. You think independently. If you listen to one news source, then you check another 5 from different viewpoints to try to understand the full picture and the agendas of each media company or political faction.

3. Focus – Specifically, focus on what you can control. With all the WMDs (weapons of mass distraction) available to us, your ability to focus and stay on a constant, strategic grind will decide whether you win or fail.

4. Action – Builders don't just sit around talking smack all day. They study, prepare, and take action. Or they seek the help of experts, not as a sign of weakness, but from a position of strength.

5. Self-Reliant – Builders don't wait on the Government or Captain Save 'Em to save them. Federal, state, and local governments may or may not be your financial friends. You may not be able to rely on anyone, except yourself.

6. Solutions, not excuses – Wealth, health, and happiness builders recognize problems and then search for solutions. Even if they have a valid excuse, they don't accept it and they plow forward since Hope is

not a Strategy.

7. KREAM – Builders realize that Knowledge Rules Everything Around Me (KREAM). So they gain financial literacy, career building/networking, and other skills. And they share this knowledge intergenerationally and without prejudice.

8. Assets vs. Liabilities – Builders understand the difference. They work to grow assets (hopefully income-producing assets) while reducing or eliminating liabilities. Builders love reinvestment of dividends over rims, growth stocks over gold chains, and cash-flowing assets over cars.

9. Producers vs. Consumers - Builders understand that to win, they have to produce more than they consume. Whether it's work product or business over social media, clothing, or other consumption, builders are always looking to put more in the Production column.

10. Passive vs Active Income - Tyreek Hill has signed a contract to make $40 million per year, which is fantastic for him and his family. This is active income because he has to be on the field to earn the income. There are real estate investors that will make $40 million this year from rental and AirBNB income, and most of the work to make this happen will be done via a property manager i.e. it will be passive income. Builders seek to maximize their active income while being mindful of opportunities to convert this active income to passive income via real estate, dividend producing stocks, insurance products, and other types of vehicles. Or they seek to create works and products that create passive income. And hopefully residual (recurring) income.

11. Long-Term vs Short-Term Thinking – Japan is over 2500 years old. China is about 3500 years old. By contrast, the United States is about 250 years old. There are advantages and disadvantages to both sides, but Builders look at both short-term opportunities and the long game. They understand that even if you may not become a millionaire

overnight, you can do it in 10 or 20 years. And you can ensure that your family grows and maintains wealth for generations.

12.Product vs. Plan – Builders understand that there are multiple financial products (like real estate, life insurance, 401ks, Roth IRAs, fixed annuities, and CDs) that they can combine, along with proper estate planning, to create an actual plan. They don't get it twisted by thinking that if they have a 401k, they have an actual plan.

13.High Expectations – Builders expect themselves and people around them to have high expectations, no matter if they're dealing with health, family, wealth building, academics, or entrepreneurial ventures. The expectation is success and failure is not an option.

14.Mentorship – Builders seek and utilize great mentors, books, and techniques to learn and advance their careers & wealth. They understand that reinventing the wheel is stupid. They seek to build on what the mentors or other resources have given them already.

15.Plans & Habits – Do you have a daily, weekly, or yearly plan? Make your bed. Do your morning exercise. Practice mindfulness techniques. Review your daily calendar. Review your weekly or annual goals. Everyone has a plan. You've either created one for yourself, or one has been created for you by friends, the media, your company, or someone else that you're currently following. I suggest you make your own.

16.Abundance vs. Scarcity - Builders see an abundance of opportunity, and realize that their biggest competition is themselves, and not other people. Builders realize that there is plenty to go around, and in fact, there is plenty more that can be created. Builders even seek alliances with competition to expand markets and grow opportunities together.

17. All That Glitters is Not Gold – In the last 5 years of observing "celebrities", if we've learned one thing it is that "all that glitters is not gold".

Do you get excited by the guy who's secretly leasing the Bentley (and posting pictures of it on Instagram), but completely miss & diss the guy driving by in a 2009 Corolla (that's paid for) who has 2 successful businesses, income-producing rental properties in multiple countries, a boatload of cash, and no financial stress? Builders aren't swayed by the glitter. They dig deeper to understand what's really going on along their path of building real wealth, health, and happiness.

CHAPTER 10

BUILDING GENERATIONAL WEALTH

If you Google the word “wealth”, it’s defined as “an abundance of valuable possessions, or money”. Search for “generational wealth”, and the definition is “wealth that gets transferred from one generation of a family to the next”.

Post-Covid, everyone agrees that we’ve now re-defined "wealth” and can assign additional meanings to it besides money including:

- Great health
- A strong network of friends & business associates
- An abundance of free time
- Unrestricted vacation time
- A healthy family or healthy children
- Freedom to do what you want

Whatever your definition of wealth is, this wealth can be developed and supported by having a rewarding career, a successful business, or a significant amount of financial assets. We will primarily focus on building the rewarding career, successful business, or financial assets that allow you to pursue your personal passions and enjoy the many types of wealth that are important to all of us now.

CHAPTER 11

FINANCIAL LITERACY & COMPETENCY

Like many Americans in general, many Black Americans don't like to talk about money. Or dying. Or taxes for that matter. In the Black American community, these discussions can be more painful or uncomfortable precisely because there is less money to talk about, less money to inherit, or less money to save on taxes. And thus, regardless of how the cycle began, the cycle of poverty, underinvestment, and lack of wealth building has continued in the Black American community.

My family is no exception. Both of my parents were well-educated masters and Ph.D holding educators who were phenomenal at their jobs. My Dad was a hard-working, beloved former administrator and principal at a county middle schools and high schools for over 30 years. If you asked my female Japanese high school students who met her in 1998 when my parents visited me in Tokyo, my Mom is a Wonder Woman who had managed to raise 2 sons, get her Ph.D, and go on to become Principal at several elementary schools for over 40 years. Both made good money, and emphasized the importance of my brother and I making great grades and going to college. But like the vast majority of Americans, both received no formal financial literacy education.

As many married couples traditionally did, one person handled the finances. In my house, My Dad did, and Mom didn't worry about things. The issue is that my Dad, in particular, did not like to talk about finances. So for 40 years, as hard-working as he was, my father did not take advantage of 401ks and other tax-deferred investment products. For 30 years, he didn't take advantage of the tax-free growth provided by Roth IRAs or cash-value life insurance products. And he didn't seek to minimize his taxes through real estate or other tax-reducing strategies. We didn't even set up an LLC for the landscaping business that we helped him run during the summer to take advantage of business deductions. And of course my brother and I didn't have any stock funds or retirement accounts set up in our names to allow us to grow our money over decades before we hit the workforce.

My Wonder Woman Mom also didn't talk about finances, not that she was particularly opposed. So for 30 years she didn't take advantage of any financial products either. Topics like her salary, her benefits, and her retirement accounts simply didn't come up in conversation. In 1999 that all changed when she and my Dad got divorced. And that's when my journey along the Financial Literacy teaching path really began. Prior to that I hadn't given any of these topics any thought. In that year we had multiple conversations about:

- Putting together funds for a down payment on a house for her
- Setting up her 401k savings products through the school district
- Reviewing her pension estimates
- Filing separate tax statements
- Life insurance
- Long-term care costs for nursing homes and home health care

I learned that we as a family hadn't put any of these plans in place, and hadn't saved anything outside of our personal real estate. And that's when the first light bulb went on.

Today, my Mom collects Social Security like tens of millions of Americans, and she is much better positioned because at that critical moment in 1999 she bravely stepped out and asked the questions. I did some research. And then we took action based on the best information available at the time. Over the years we've refined the strategy to include the following:

- IRAs
- CD's
- Fixed Indexed Annuities
- Whole life insurance (funded by required minimum distributions from her old 401k)
- A long-term care insurance plan that will cover costs
- Pre-paid burial costs

- A will and estate plan, along with health care and financial power of attorney directives

I am determined to never let this happen again within my family, and this type of research followed by ACTION is exactly what we're going to bring to the table for Black America (and any Americans that want to get their stuff together).

Actions speak louder than words, so by contrast, my daughter has already heard the words:

- Stocks
- Dividends
- Real estate
- Assets
- Insurance
- Taxes

And she's also gotten a lesson in inflation already. I took her to the Dollar Tree, and the "dollar" has now changed to $1.25, so I had to explain to her that she could only buy 2 items with the $3.25 in quarters that she dug out of my side door due to inflation. That discussion didn't make her too happy.

By the time she is 10 she will be:

- Reviewing her stock portfolio
- Selecting her own stocks, ETFs, and REITs to buy
- Giving me a report on dividends associated with those stocks
- Reviewing her whole life insurance policy values

and figuring out the taxes due on items she buys in stores.

And she will understand these key definitions:

- Budgeting – Adding up personal revenues, adding up personal expenses, understanding what's left over every month, and then understanding what you can spend or invest in
- Compounding – the process in which earnings are reinvested to generate additional earnings over time. Compounding works

both ways (positively and negatively), and can be done daily, weekly, monthly, or annually. Builders work on positive compounding (of interest, dividends, job gains, real estate earnings, networking gains) on a daily, weekly, monthly, and annual basis.

- Automation – In a wealth building sense, automation is about setting up income from the job, business, or from other earnings to invest automatically at set intervals. Automation takes the effort out of investing and can guarantee the successful building of wealth over time.

Builders realize that though these topics aren't initially "sexy", they're important enough to either:

A. Master on your own
B. Outsource the decision making to an expert
C. Seek out mentors or advisors to seek guidance from

And they realize that they need to pass this information both down the generational line and up the generational line.

CHAPTER 12

THE FIVE THIEVES REVISITED

No, this isn't a chapter on a new fine wine called the "4 Thieves". And this isn't a movie premiere. These 4 thieves are decidedly less sexy, and much more pernicious. The 4 things that can rob you of wealth (and momentum) are: 1. Taxes 2. Fees 3. Inflation 4. Weapons of Mass Distraction.

You'll get a 100x return from this book if you focus on any of the 5 Thieves. If you find an answer for all 5, or use experts to help you find the answers, you're golden. And you'll become wealthy.

TAXES

- Why the heck are you paying all these taxes?
- What do you get for paying all these freaking taxes?
- Should you move somewhere where you aren't paying all these doggone taxes?
- Is it worth it to stay in your country, state, city, or county and pay the taxes they demand?

If you live in a high income tax state, and the city or county also happens to charge municipality income taxes or even high property taxes, then you have to do math on whether the juice is worth the squeeze. In other words, is the ROI (return on your investment) worth all of that tax? Are you better off staying in that jurisdiction than moving to a new one? Are you getting your tax money's worth? These are all key questions that any Builder must ask.

FEES

Same drill. Ask yourself:

- Why the heck am I paying all these fees?

- What do I get for paying all these freaking fees?
- Should you move your money somewhere where you aren't paying all these dang fees?
- Regarding non-financial management fees, have you reviewed all the fees included on your cable, utility, and phone bills? And what the hell is the government or the company doing with all those fees?

Standard mutual funds charge between 0.5% - 1.5% per year, regardless of the performance of the mutual funds. Standard financial advisors and planners charge the same. Sometimes those fees are added together for annual fees of 1 – 3%. If you are paying fees, you should let an expert analyze what you're paying them for, and get your money's worth.

The ROI calculation applies: Am I getting superior performance in return for these higher fees, or am I better served putting my money in a stock market index vehicle?

INFLATION: THE STEALTH TAX

When inflation is 1-2% a year, it's not a big deal, right? How about when it's 9% a year? If you're familiar with the Rule of 72, you know that's a BFD (big friggin deal) since your buying power is evaporating at a 9% clip every year. Over the next 2 decades, Americans may face inflation in the 5-10% range.

Are you:

- Increasing your salary by 5-10% a year?
- Realizing 5-10% investment gains every year?
- Reducing your expenses by 5-10% a year?

Don't believe we're experiencing inflation. Then why did Dollar Tree "break the dollar" and go to $1.25? I rest my case.

VOLATILITY & INCONSISTENT RETURNS

Volatility and inconsistent returns are the enemies of building and preserving wealth.

If you're working and accumulating assets by contributing to your portfolio, you can potentially recover from market swings while DCA'ing (dollar cost averaging in) to get more shares cheaper when the market is down. may be able to recover from these market swings.

But once you stop working and start relying on your life savings to fund your income in retirement, this is a completely different mindset that requires a shift in thinking and a shift in skills needed (either internally or from experts that you hire to work for you).

Inconsistent returns also disrupt compounding growth. For example, if you experience a 50% loss one year, you need a 100% gain just to get back to where you started. This reality makes it difficult to sustain long-term growth, and have a reliable income in retirement.

For wealth builders, reducing volatility is critical. The Year 2025+ strategies and products that are different from the 1950's era "buy and hold stocks and bonds" mantras are required for:

- True diversification
- Tax efficiency
- Consistent Growth
- Risk Reduction

WMDs:

(Weapons of Mass Distraction)

In a span of 10 days in 2022 the former president questioned the narrative of 9/11, Nancy Pelosi gave China the greatest weapon of mass distraction for beaten down Chinese people in 25 years by going to Taiwan, and the current President tried to redefine the definition of a recession. And, oh yeah, a former President had his mansion raided. And that's not even close to all the stuff that happened in that 10-day span like the ongoing war with Ukraine, the ending of legal abortion in the US, and monkeypox to name a few other tidbits.

I used to spend 2 hours every morning consuming news and media to "educate" myself on what was going on. What a tremendous waste of time. And a what a stressor.

Is your pronoun game strong (she/her, him/he, they/them)? Do you know the definition of gaslighting, cisgender, etc.? But you have no idea what an ETF, REIT, MLP, or P/E ratio is? And you have no strategy for how to build wealth? There is no wonder why this may be the case.

How the hell can you deal with politics, gender wars, racial issues, and all other WMDs, and still have enough time, energy, and focus to build health, wealth, and happiness? (This is a trick question. You can't.)

The solution? Decide what's actually important to you (not anyone or anything else), and then prioritize your time, energy, and focus on that. Simply put, You should spend a maximum of 1 hour a day on the following WMDs:

- Network news
- Social media
- Videos
- Newspapers
- Email
- Texts or calls from family & friends

And unless you run your business through your phone, you shouldn't spend more than an hour a day on it.

Why? Because you are your most valuable asset, time is your most valuable resource, and you have things to do!

What can you spend your time on instead?

- Working out
- Working (intelligently) and hopefully in batch mode (doing the same thing for 3 hours at a time)
- Meditating
- Planning your day

- Reviewing or creating your goals
- Spending quality time with your family (without devices)
- Sleeping
- Hitting the sauna
- Getting some sun
- Figuring out how to create other businesses
- Reviewing your investments
- Reviewing investment options

So, put that phone down, turn off that TV, and focus. Why? Because you've got building to do!

CHAPTER 13

THE WEALTH BUILDER'S BLUEPRINT

Ready to get started on the path towards building your dreams in a traditional career or in a startup or entrepreneurial venture? Here's the guide on how to maximize your career and to build generational wealth and happiness:

1. **The What:** What are you passionate about and can become the best in the world at? Or what business would you like to build?
    a. To find out, take a career assessment. Multiple ones are available including the Birkman, the U.S. O*Net Interest Profiler, & the Pathsource Assessment.
    b. Do research on specific internships & co-ops available, and seek the experience.
    c. Research and consult with friends, family, and your network on job opportunities.

2. **The What's Going On**: Before you dive into any industry, you need to:
    a. Review the prospects and outlook for the industry (what are current challenges, opportunities, etc.)
    b. Do a deep dive on Megatrends that are affecting all industries.
    c. These Megatrends include:
        i. Artificial Intelligence
        ii. Automation/Robotics
        iii. Virtual Reality/Metaverse Development
        iv. Electric Vehicles
        v. Cryptocurrency/Blockchain development
        vi. Cybersecurity challenges
        vii. Global trade/supply chain challenges
        viii. Global Tech Workforce Mobility
        ix. Environmental Sciences/Sustainability

x. Healthcare/Longevity Innovation

xi. The Silver Tsunami (the graying of the population)

3. **The How**: Skills Development for any job

   a. To become the best in the world, you'll need mastery of many of these skills including:

      i. The Ability to Learn & Ability to Adapt

      ii. English (or your native language) (spoken, written, & reading)

      iii. Basic Math

      iv. Critical Thinking/Questioning

      v. Digital Literacy & Coding: Basic coding skill regardless of path (blockchain, digital design)

      vi. The Entrepreneurial Mindset i.e. Can you think like a Boss? Do you understand profit & loss?

      vii. Financial Literacy

      viii. Negotiation

      ix. Sales/Self-Promotion/Marketing

4. **The Decision**: Picking the certification program, university, the graduate school, etc. (if necessary) to take your skills to the next level

   a. What is the success rate of the school? Specifically, use this website to find the answers to the following questions: https://nces.ed.gov/collegenavigator/

      i. What is the 4-year graduation rate?

      ii. What is the average salary 6 months out of school?

      iii. What % of graduates have jobs 6 months after graduation?

   b. How much debt will you accumulate to go to the school?

   c. What is the typical ROI (return on investment) for the school? Specifically,

      i. What is the average salary vs. average student loan ratio?

ii. How long does it take for the average graduate to pay off their loans?

d. What is the ROT (return on time) for going to the school (i.e. how much more will you make by getting the certification, degree, etc.)?

e. What networks will you have access to in school and after you leave?

f. Is your school in the right city or region for your future career?

5. **The Job**: How can you maximize your opportunities and development at the job?

6. **Expected Cash Flow & Benefits**

a. Expected Income: How much will you get paid for that job (or running that business)?

b. Salary & Job Negotiations: How can you a) get the job? and b) negotiate aggressively for your best interests on the front end? There are multiple resources available to help.

c. The Benefits – How do you pick the right benefits? Please see the "How to Pick the Right Benefits" guide.

7. **The Location**

a. What city, state, or country should you locate in to launch your career or business? Please see the "How to Pick the Right City" guide.

i. Is it growing?

ii. Can you take advantage of the network in that city?

iii. How many large/growing companies does city have (S&P 1000, Inc. 5000 list)?

1. Are those companies hiring? If so, for what positions & how much?

2. What are the growth prospects with those companies?

8. **The Start Up or Side Hustle**: Can you grow a business on the side while you work (or during school)? Do you want to go for the gold and start a business right away?

a. What are your long-term goals for:
   i. A career
   ii. A possible business
   iii. Financial freedom/wealth building
   iv. Family/social life
   v. Life after the career or business

b. How much experience do you have in the business or side hustle?

c. Are you passionate about creating your own business?

d. Is it a growing sector?

e. Is it a business that you can innovate in i.e. what's your unique advantage?

f. Find a mentor in real life or online (podcasts, books, videos) that you can learn from

g. Write a 1-page business plan, and sell it to your friends, family. This may improve the plan.

h. How you will get the first customers?
   i. How much will you charge?
   ii. How will you make $?

i. Timetable for launch: When are you going to start selling or offering the service? Can you build an MVP (minimally viable product) to launch early?

j. Will your business produce:
   i. Residual income?
   ii. Passive income?

9. **What to do with The $$$**: The Path to Generational Wealth & Happiness What do you do now that you've started earning $$$ from your career or business?

a. Financial Literacy & Investing Basics: Review the Employee Benefit Guide in later chapters and learn the basics on budgeting, 401ks, IRAs /IRA basics, etc.

b. The Roth IRA: Can you max it out? If you can, consider doing so.

c. Investing for Cash Flow? Some ideas include:

   i. Real estate

   ii. Dividend-producing stocks

d. Will your investments produce:

   i. Residual income?

   ii. Passive income?

e. The Rainy Day Fund: Build 6 months of savings.

f. Excess Funds: Ideas for investment can include:

   i. Purchasing additional dividend-producing stocks, REITs, and ETFs

   ii. Purchasing growth stocks

   iii. Investing in Cash-Value Whole Life Insurance vehicles

   iv. Cryptocurrency

   v. Alternative investments like farmland or wine

   vi. Private equity & Start up investments

   vii. Real Estate Crowdfunding platforms

   viii. Short-term rental purchases

g. Tax & Fee Reduction:

   i. Mind your pence and cents (review the fees in your retirement and investment accounts in your mutual funds, etc.)

   ii. Review your taxes every year with a tax accountant to legally minimize them

   iii. Set up a business or purchase real estate each year to reduce taxes?

10. **The Fun!**

a. Where do you want to vacation or spend time with your friends, family?

b. Can you take some "business before pleasure" trips where you get both in and learn about a new city, country, etc.?

As always, do your own research. Have Fun! And Build!

TO COLLEGE OR NOT TO COLLEGE? THAT IS THE QUESTION

A general understanding of financial literacy, passive income vs. active income, assets over liabilities, and The 5 Thieves can greatly and intelligently dictate your choice of both career and whether or not to go to college. If you do decide to go to college, this financial literacy education may dictate which college and city you decide to invest both your hard-earned money and time in.

Make no mistake about it. Picking the right college or school to invest your time, money, and soul into can make or break your overall career. So picking a school close to home, just because it's close to home for example, is NOT a good enough reason to go to that school.

As a "superstar" coming out of one of the nation's top 25 high schools I applied to 8 schools across the East Coast, Midwest, and Southeast, and got into all 8. My goal had always been to go to college because my Dad told me that's where I needed to go. I didn't know there was another option.

And I wanted to become a doctor because that's what my Dad told me I should become. That made sense since I was great in biology. Had I ever really met any doctors? No. Had I ever spent any time shadowing doctors? No. Did I know all the different types of positions physicians could have? No. Did I know the full process on how to become a doctor? No. And had I taken any sort of career assessment to tell me whether I had the aptitude or desire to become a doctor? Of course not.

On the basis of this lack of information, I chose a prestigious school within 3 hours of my hometown that seemed cool, had a great pre-med program, and was giving me a full academic scholarship and allowing me to play football. I was the Big Man on campus at my high school, and I fully expected that status to be maintained at Morehouse College in Atlanta, Georgia.

Morehouse & Atlanta were revelations to my brain, and I definitely wasn't fully prepared to handle either one during my freshman year. I made decent grades but dropped off the football team after a big rumble with a teammate. Dropping that habit (of working out constantly and being part of something bigger than myself) had a big negative impact on my self identity.

But at the end of the first year of classes, a real doctor came into to speak to us and show us slides of his work at Howard University Medical Center. And that is a day that will live in infamy. He showed us crazy slides of injuries, car crash victims, burn victims, and more that he courageously dealt with and repaired. The personal "favorite" that put me "over the top" was a homeless man who had come in with a knife lodged between his mouth and his right ear.

That day I decided that I had no idea what I was going to do with my life, but that I wasn't going to do any of that. I had no thoughts of looking into being a different type of doctor, or an anesthesiologist or anything like that. That day my career goal of becoming a doctor went up in smoke, never to return.

A year later, after taking a part-time job to make some money so I could live off-campus (big mistake), and after half-assing my way through a business major for the year, I lost my scholarship, and went from "high school superstar" to college dropout rapidly and unceremoniously.

I eventually came back, with the help of $27,000 in student loans, not because of my own guidance, but because of the guidance and support of a few influential mentors I had access to at the time. With those mentors, along with Dr. John Handy, a tremendous & sometimes combative Finance & Economics professor who challenged me and woke me up from my "coma", I re-enrolled, excelled, and graduated with honors on time. My journey through university ended up fine, as has my career, but it could have been greatly enhanced by the process I'm going to share here. I started with 900 other freshmen, and graduated with 334, or so.

My hope is that whether you're a future college student, a parent, or even a future grad school student, you will NOT reinvent the wheel. Just make it better. Please review the process and the "How to Pick a College" guide to fast track your way to success.

HOW TO PICK THE BEST COLLEGE/UNIVERSITY/ SCHOOL/CERTIFICATE OR TRADE PROGRAM

Do you need to go to college? Are you sure? 100%? Because it can be expensive!

If so, does it have to be 4-year or can it be 2-year?

When you finish, how much $$ will you make going to make, and will that be enough to survive?

What if you got a certificate or trade certification instead of a 4-year degree? How much faster or slower can you attain millionaire status (i.e. how much more or less money will you save and invest over the first 15 years of your career)?

Have you considered a gap year (a year between high school and/or graduate school and a higher education) to make sure you have your stuff together?

Have you considered geographic educational arbitrage (going somewhere across the country where there are only a few people from your state and where the university will give you more money simply to have your representative state/background in the building)?

Did you know you may be able to attend university in Germany, Brazil, and Norway for free?

Did you know you can attend university and graduate school in Canada for a fraction of the cost of attending school in the United States?

Do you realize there are programs that will pay you to go to undergrad and graduate school in Japan?

If you took the $70,000 per year for 4 years that some students will spend to go to American universities and either invested it in dividend-producing stocks or in a franchise business, would you be better off than the average college graduate 10 years from now?

And has anyone ever asked you or told you any of this?

The College Decision Making Process:

a. What is the success rate of the school? Specifically, use this website to find the answers to the following questions: https://nces.ed.gov/collegenavigator/
   i. What is the 4-year graduation rate?
   ii. What is the average salary 6 months out of school?
   iii. What % of graduates have jobs 6 months after graduation?

b. How much debt will you accumulate to go to the school?

c. What is the typical ROI (return on investment) for the school? Specifically,
   i. What is the average salary vs. average student loan ratio?
   ii. How long does it take for the average graduate to pay off their loans?

d. What is the ROT (return on time) for going to the school (i.e. how much more will you make by getting the certification, degree, etc.)?

e. What networks will you have access to in school and after you leave?

f. Is your school in the right city or region for your future career?

I'm pro-college and anti-college, depending on the person, situation, and cost. The point is to not just blindly follow what other people tell you to do, or what your friends are doing. Weigh the options, do some math, and then make a more informed decision

HOW TO PICK A CITY (*seriously*)

Why do you live where you live?

Is it the best place in the world for you to live? Why?

If it isn't, are you going to stay there, are you going to adjust to the realities of being there, or are you going to do something more about it?

One of the most important decisions in your life is deciding where to live, start your career, and invest your money, energy, and time into. Too many of us spend too little time thinking about where we currently live, or where we may need to live, to achieve our life and financial dreams. After working in over 20 industries, traveling to 25 countries, doing business with 30+ nationalities, working for 30 years, visiting over 155 major cities worldwide, and visiting 1,000+ smaller towns, I've created the blueprint for How to pick the best place to live. Also, please notice that I'm intentional about saying that a city may NOT be the best place for you. A smaller town or even village may be the best place for you to build your foundation. You need to know yourself, understand your likely career or entrepreneurial path, and then use this guide to help you pick the best spot possible on Earth.

How to Pick the Best City/Town: The Keys

Economy & Population

- GDP – Is the economy growing?
  - ▸Is it growing faster than the national GDP rate?
  - ▸Is the MSA (metropolitan statistical area) or municipal area's population shrinking or expanding? And at what percentage (%)?
  - ▸What are the latest business/economic development announcements in the region (i.e. Are companies moving to the region? If so, why?? Or are companies leaving the region? If so, why???!)
  - ▸What's the export activity of the city/town? What % of city GDP is created from exports?

Jobs

- Job Market
  - ▸Unemployment rate
  - ▸Average monthly/yearly income
  - ▸Average hourly earnings growth (last 12 months)
  - ▸Jobs available online
  - ▸Jobs available for remote work
- Companies
  - ▸How many large or growing companies does the city have (on the Fortune 500, S&P 1000, Inc. 5000, or top 1000 Private companies list)?
    - Are those companies hiring or expanding?
    - If so, for which positions, and what are the salaries?
    - What are the growth prospects with those companies either by working for them or starting a business that can partner with them?
    - Are there any industry clusters (i.e. IT startups in Silicon Valley) in the city?

- Megatrends

  ‣Are any companies in these cities leaders in megatrends (large shifts in industry or potentially huge industries) including:

    - Artificial Intelligence
    - Automation/Robotics
    - Virtual Reality/Metaverse Development
    - Electric Vehicles
    - Cryptocurrency/Blockchain development
    - Cybersecurity
    - Global trade/supply chain challenges
    - Global Tech Workforce Mobility
    - Environmental Sciences/Sustainability
    - Healthcare/Longevity Innovation
    - The Silver Tsunami (the graying of the population)

- Network

  ‣Can you take advantage of the Chamber of Commerce, university, professional, etc. network in the region?

  ‣Can you be a contrarian and take advantage of the smaller network in a smaller city (become a big fish in a small pond)?

- Livability

  a. The Arts

    - What artistic or creative activity is going on in the city/town? Creative activity can precede economic prosperity.

- Housing

  b. Housing Prices

    - What is the average cost of a home in the city?
    - What's the annual real estate appreciation (housing increase) %?

  c. Rent Affordability

    - Average Rent in the city
    - What is the percentage (%) of increase in annual rents over the last 2 years?
    - Do you need to find roommates to make it work?

- Crime
    a. What are the violent crime rates per capita?
    b. If you're female, will you feel safe in this city?
    c. Crime trends: Is the crime rate going up or down? Last year? 3 years ago?

- Traffic & Logistics
    a. What's the average commute?
    b. Is there abundant public transportation?
    c. Is there rail or light rail available?
    d. High-speed rail connections to other cities available?
    e. The airport
        - Direct domestic flights?
            - How many and to where?
        - Direct International Flights?
            - How many and to where?
- Planning & Politics
    - ▸Is the city dysfunctional, or does it seem to have its act together?
    - ▸Does the city have a strategic plan that is being followed, or is it just drifting?
        - If so, how are they doing with implementing the plan? Are the metrics improving or declining? Do they even track metrics? If they don't, this can be a big red flag since this might mean that they don't care what the tax money collected is being used for.
- Taxes
    - ▸ Are all these taxes above or below the national average? Or even non-existent?
    - ▸Does the local government think of you as an asset or as an ATM?
    - ▸Performance vs. Taxes – how is the state, city, county doing?
    - ▸Do they have a state income tax?
    - ▸Do they have a municipal income tax?

- ▸Do they have a commuter income tax?
- ▸Does the state or city have a corporate income tax?
- ▸Sales taxes – Are they above or below the national average?
  - Local taxes
  - State taxes
  - Hospitality taxes
- ▸Property taxes(if you are going to own your home)
  - Personal home tax rates?
  - Commercial property tax rates (if they're outrageous commercial taxes companies may be hesitant to invest in that city)
  - Auto and auto registration taxes and fees

- Fun - What resources and options below are available in the region? And do people love visiting the region? Does the region host a lot of conventions? Is the number of conventions going up or down?
  - ▸Bars
  - ▸Restaurants
  - ▸Museums
  - ▸Parks
  - ▸Concert Halls
  - ▸Theaters
  - ▸Professional Sports Teams
  - ▸College Teams
  - ▸Music Venues
  - ▸Famous types of food?
  - ▸Breweries
  - ▸Wineries
  - ▸Zoos
  - ▸Kids' activities (do they have them, are they expensive, are they easy?)

- Climate Change

Forget the politics. You better study the actual trends & information in the area you're looking to move to, especially if you plan on purchasing a house or other real estate there. Here are some practical questions to ask yourself about the area or real estate in the area in general:

- Does it flood often?
- Can I purchase property at a higher elevation or in a non-flood zone?
- What is the likelihood of forest fires or soil erosion?
- How much have property & casualty insurance companies increased home insurance rates in the last 5 years? You may have to contact an insurance agency to get this data.
- Can you even get insurance in that city?
- How many natural disasters have hit the neighborhood/city/state in the last 10 years?
- What type of structure should I buy (brick, reinforced steel, concrete, etc.)?
- What sort of roofing does it have? Can it withstand a hurricane, tornado, etc.?

CHAPTER 14

THE NAME GAME

What's in a name? Is wealth in a name? Is the potential for irrelevance and generational poverty in a name? Have you ever heard of **Issur Danielovitch Demsky**?

Of course you haven't! Why? Because that was a hard-ass name to pronounce. So, what did Issur do? He changed his name. Not his looks. Not his talent. Not his intelligence. Just his name.

And by doing so, he rebranded himself in a way that contributed to his immense success. Today, we know him as Kirk Douglas. We know his son as Michael Douglas. And we now know their family as one of the wealthiest and most well-powerful names in Hollywood.

Names carry weight. They shape perceptions, open doors, and even create or close off opportunities. In the world of wealth-building, names can be more than labels—they can be assets.

On a personal note, my name is Benjamin.

When I first arrived in Japan, I introduced myself as "Ben." A simple choice, I thought, but one that soon proved problematic.

In Spain, I also initially introduced myself as "Ben." But then I learned that in Spanish, "Benjamín" refers to a small bottle of champagne. I found this amusing but not particularly impactful.

However, during my second stint in Japan, I decided to dig deeper. I wanted to understand how my name might be interpreted in this cultural context. What I discovered was... illuminating.

The Japanese language is rich with homophones—words that sound the same but have vastly different meanings. Depending on the context, "Ben" in Japanese can mean:

- **Convenient** (benri)
- **Study** (benkyo)

- **Lawyer** (bengoshi)
- **Toilet** (benjo)
- Or, less politely, **excrement**.

You can imagine my surprise—and discomfort—when I realized the potential interpretations of my name.

But there was a silver lining. I learned that "Benjamin," when pronounced phonetically in Japanese as "Ben-ji-man," closely resembles the phrase "Benevolent 10,000." This phrase connotes abundance, generosity, and goodness. What a stark contrast to the unintended meanings of "Ben"!

Moreover, "Benjamin" has another connection in Japan: the Benjamin fig tree, known locally as "Benjamina." This tree is admired for its elegance, its sweet aroma, and its impressive stature, reaching heights of nearly two meters. It's also celebrated as an excellent air purifier.

Armed with this knowledge, I had a choice to make: stick with "Ben," a name that risked awkward misinterpretations like "toilet" and "poop", or embrace "Benjamin," a name that resonated with positivity, growth, abundance, occasional femininity, and sweet smells.

I'll let you guess which one I chose.

In Japan the choice had significant positive impacts on my business prospects, my career, and even my dating life (*smiling face emoji*).

The Wealth-Building Lesson

Names matter—whether they're your own, your business's, or even a product's. They set the tone for how people perceive you and what you represent.

Think about it: Would you buy a luxury car named "Clunker"? Or invest in a financial advisor whose name conjures images of failure?

The same principle applies to wealth-building. Your name and your brand should reflect the values, aspirations, and success you aim to achieve. Sometimes, that means rebranding to better align with your goals.

Think about some people that are considered the "GOATs" (greatest or most notable of all time) in their respective careers?

- Billionaire Businessmen and women – Bill, Warren, Elon, Oprah, Jeff, Larry, Robert, Steve
- Basketball – Mike, Steph, Shaq, Kobe, Larry, Bill, Wilt, Lebron
- Female Vocalist or Entertainer – Whitney, Aretha, Mariah, Ella, Billie, Taylor, Celine (the only outlier is Beyonce')
- Football – Tom, Patrick, Walter, Dick, Earl, Reggie
- Baseball – Babe, Hank, Reggie
- Boxing – Mike, Ali
- Male Singer or Entertainer – Michael, Frank, Elvis, Bob, Prince, James, Jimi, Bob, Otis, Marvin, Stevie, Sting (no one has more than two syllables)
- Female Actresses – Halle, Meryl, Audrey, Scarlett (Angela, Katharine, & Marilyn are the only ones with more than 2 syllables)
- Male Actors & Directors – Marlon, Humphrey, Leo, Ben, Matt, Robert, Al, Denzel, Tom, Spike, Jack, Kirk, Michael (Samuel is the only one with 3 syllables)
- Rappers & Producers – BIG, 2Pac, Jay-Z, Nas, 50, Rakim, Snoop, Dre, Lil Wayne, Rick Ross, Ye', Cube, Kendrick, Drake, LL, Ja, Game (Rap has the most outliers or famous names that are more than two syllables with Eminem, Run DMC, EPMD, Marley Marl, Curtis Blow, and Big Daddy Kane as examples). Even the very "non-PC" name Fat Joe has worked well.

How about notable businesses?

- Coke.
- Nike.
- Ford.
- GM.
- Tesla.
- Zoom.
- Twitter.
- Uber.
- Visa.
- Facebook.

All of these names are brilliant…in their simplicity and ease of pronunciation.

Need I go on? And how many of these folks above have names longer than 2 syllables? Only a few.

Even the name GOD is simple. 3 letters. No chances of mispronunciation, misspelling, or mistakes. You can't get any simpler than G-O-D.

I rest my case.

Whether you're deciding what to name your business, your book, or even how to present yourself in a different culture, consider the power of perception. A name isn't just a label; it's a wealth and career building opportunity. And in the game of building generational wealth, every opportunity counts.

CHAPTER 15

PIMP YOUR CAREER

GLOBAL SUPERSTAR™ SKILLS: THE DIFFERENTIATORS

Whatever you do, and no matter where you end up in the world, you'll need basic skills out that were hopefully mastered in high school to succeed. In the following chapter we explore the skill sets required to blow it out of the water and achieve your dreams.

THE DIFFERENCE MAKERS

What skills will 5x your opportunities, especially after Covid, and in light of the megatrends of Talent Migration, Global Workforce Availability, and the growing use of Artificial Intelligence?

AN EXCELLENT COMMAND OF ENGLISH

This is a simple, yet important skill to have, and more difficult to come by every day with the advent of instant messaging and social media like including Twitter and Facebook, along with a general drop in readership of books. This is the most obvious differentiator, and yet the one that may be most taken for granted in English-speaking countries. On a daily basis, you can encounter business reports, correspondence, and even articles written by Americans, Britons, Australians, or Canadians that exhibit worse grammar and spelling skills than many people who were born and raised in China, Argentina, or the Netherlands exhibit. Here's the bottom line: If your native English-speaking kids can't read, write, or speak proper English, why would someone hire them over a nonnative speaker that can communicate in English better, speaks at least one more language, may have a better work ethic, and may do the job for a lower salary?

This may sound harsh, but it's the exact thinking of many American, Canadian, and European manufacturers and corporations when they make decisions on where create jobs. Rising costs around the world in many offshoring centers and increased shipping costs mean many of these jobs stand a good chance of coming back to North America. But United States and Canadian graduates will still have to compete with their counterparts in Mexico. In the European Union, these jobs are unlikely to come back, so their college graduates may be even hungrier to compete for jobs going forward. If these jobs come back, children and young adults in the United States and Canada will have to be ready to compete for these opportunities. If they're not ready and there is a shortage of talent like Manpower has forecasted, then these corporations will take these jobs to other countries with talented labor pools.

AN EXCELLENT COMMAND OF BASIC MATH SKILLS

Being able to add, subtract, multiply, and divide numbers quickly and without the help of a calculator is crucial and increasingly rare these days. Basic math skills will give you an advantage in life and business.

CRITICAL THINKING and QUESTIONING SKILLS

Politics aside, you must be able to ingest material from all sides, do your own research, and come up with your own conclusions or additional questions to ask. This will serve you well in life, and in your career.

ORGANIZATION and PRIORITIZATION SKILLS

You have must be able to prioritize tasks and set steps to accomplish tasks. If you can prioritize and organize work for others, this is even better, and will put you in line for leadership positions. One way to do this is by taking project management courses or getting project management certifications.

SPEAKING SKILLS

Speaking classes, debate, or drama club--all of these activities will develop their ability to command an audience (i.e., speak with their staff or peers), and it will help them overcome a fear of speaking in front of others. People who can speak in front of an audience in a confident, competent manner have an instant advantage over their counterparts (in any country). Being able to confidently and competently deliver short arguments, presentations or other speeches in front of an audience, no matter the size, will set your child apart from most. If they can also sprinkle in a bit of wit or show their personality during the delivery, the audience will be even more enraptured.

BASIC LEGAL KNOWLEDGE

A business law class in high school, at a two-year college or university, or an online business legal course can help immensely. In the United States in particular, virtually everything comes with a written or unwritten contract. The European Union countries aren't far behind the United States in terms of being legally burdensome. Whether you are negotiating for a job, putting down an offer on a home, or negotiating for more pickles on your cheeseburger, a basic legal background will go a long way. This is in addition to the next recommendation which can also put you ahead of the pack.

NEGOTIATION SKILLS

That's right baby. Negotiation skills. Because every interaction we have with another human being involves some form of negotiation. Every interaction.

Whether it's to negotiate who's going to take out the trash, asking that person you like out for a date, or asking your child to never again use that colorful magic marker on the walls in your house, everything involves negotiation. I spent 12 years in secondary education, four years in university, four years working overseas in three countries, and even a year in business school before I took a course called "Negotiation." When I finally took the course, the ubiquity of negotiations became clear to me. Don't wait that long to formally study the concept of negotiation. Check out some negotiation books from the library, or listen to some podcasts or audio books on negotiation. You will get your money and time back 100x over from studying negotiations.

Recommended reading for improving negotiation skills: "Getting to Yes" by Roger Fisher and William Ury.

SALES SKILLS

Why? Because like negotiation, everyone sells everything. And everything involves sales. The sooner your kids realize this, the better. Whether it's attending a sales seminar, reading a sales book, or talking to someone in a direct sales role, your kids or students should familiarize themselves with the concept and process of sales. As you're reviewing negotiation, you'll be thinking of the sales process as well. And if you can get them sales experience early on (through a lemonade stand, a small entrepreneurial venture, etc.), then that's even better.

TECHNOLOGY and DIGITAL LITERACY SKILLS

You will benefit greatly from:

- "Fluency" in the MS Office suite (Word, Excel, PowerPoint, and Access later down the line), including knowing keyboard shortcuts will help tremendously, and save you time.
- "Fluency" in using Apple® products, including Mac and iPad, or Android® phones and tablets.
- "Fluency" with digital communications platforms like Facebook messenger, Gmail, and Skype.
- Experience with online meetings or calls using technologies like Zoom, Microsoft Teams, FaceTime, Google Hangout or Skype.
- Familiarization with Customer relationship management systems like Salesforce.com or Nimble.
- Familiarization with LinkedIn.
- Basic-to-moderate graphic design and content design skills (the more, the better).

Where can you learn these skills for free?

You can try your local library, or these resources:

- Khan Academy website
- Microsoft's Digital Literacy website
- Google's Web Curriculum website

EQ (EMOTIONAL INTELLIGENCE)

Whether it's the ability to empathize, knowing when to provide words of comfort to employees, or knowing when to shut up and let someone else talk, emotional intelligence is essential for any leader of a company. You can each the top of the hill without a great EQ, but you may have trouble staying at the top or getting any of your team to help along the way without empathetic abilities. Students coming out of India and China in particular have historically had challenges developing these EQ and soft skills. These skills will continue to represent a challenge for some, while representing an advantage for graduates competing against them who make the effort to develop EQ abilities.

ENTREPRENEURIAL SKILLS

The official Webster's definition of an entrepreneur is "one who organizes, manages, and assumes the risks of a business or enterprise." Even if your kids work for companies their entire lives, they'll do better if they have the attitude and skill set of an entrepreneur.

Entrepreneurship can be risky, but thinking your corporate or government job is safe can be risky too. And outside of political and military leaders, the world has been most significantly impacted by entrepreneurs. Jeff Bezos, Bill Gates, Warren Buffett, Masayoshi Son, Kim Kardashian, Riyanna, Richard Branson, Sam Walton, Mark Zuckerberg, Mark Cuban, Jay-Z, Silvio Berlusconi, Dr. Dre, Magic Johnson, Sara Blakely, Michael Jordan, Carlos Slim, Rosalia Mera, Steve Jobs, Steve Harvey, Tyler Perry, George Lucas, Ingvar Kamprad, Oprah Winfrey, and Elon Musk are all examples of entrepreneurs that have had huge impacts on the world--and this is only a short list of notable ones.

Successful entrepreneurs can also make a ton of money (as have all of these people listed), so don't reinvent the entire wheel! Study entrepreneurs that interest you, and recognize the opportunities you have to become an accomplished entrepreneur yourself. And with the ongoing challenge university graduates have in finding great paying jobs after school, what's one way that you can improve your employment situation? You can create your own job!

ABILITY TO ENJOY DIFFERENT FOODS

Hopefully you weren't expecting to get just standard advice from this book, so this is one more example of a "soft skill" that can go a long way towards lifetime success. You can look like a star and make people gawk in wonder over your ability to not just try, but enjoy their local delicacies in the different countries or the different regions of the North America that you visit. Many people from around the world think Americans and Brits have a limited palate (i.e., we only eat hamburgers and fish and chips). The ability to try different types of food without cringing can take you a long way when you're in Shanghai and they plop some "stinky" tofu in front of you, or when you're in Tokyo and they want to see if the foreigner can stomach sashimi. And never underestimate the power of "beer diplomacy" to deepen business relationships and make you a ton of money. The ability to enjoy the local food and drink instead of just heading to the nearest McDonald's can separate you from others, and put business partners and staff that you will have to deal with overseas at ease more quickly, especially in today's environment .

If you can gain the confidence to grab the menu from your host while you're on business in their country and pick a few local favorites off the menu that everybody will enjoy, that will impress your hosts even more. It works like a charm.

CONFLICT RESOLUTION SKILLS

There's no need for to explain the importance of this skill. The ability to dive into challenges or conflicts with colleagues, staff or others head on and talk through issues in a competent, calm manner will be very valuable going forward.

Recommended reading: "Crucial Conversations: Tools for Talking When Stakes Are High" by Kerry Patterson, Joseph Grenny, Ron McMillan and Al Switzler.

BUSINESS ETIQUETTE

From choosing the right fork for the salad, to knowing how to shake hands and exchange business cards, or learning to look people in the eye when in conversation, building the basics of business etiquette will help you during the course of your career. There may be business etiquette classes at university, or private classes or programs around your town that can give yourself greater exposure to these skills. Or just check it out on YouTube.

FINANCIAL LITERACY

You must be armed with the basics of personal finance, either through books, workbooks or formal classes. Basic knowledge of investments and profit/loss statements will help you have a more comprehensive view of any company's operations that you join. An in-depth understanding of profit and loss statements, or revenue and expenses, will also give you a heads up on how the company is doing and whether you should look for a new job or create your own job. Finally, a general knowledge of retirement planning principles and vehicles will help you in your salary and compensation negotiations. And it will help you lay a solid path towards building generational wealth while cutting your taxable income. Or you'll be able to set up a tax-free retirement down the line, which may be even better.

PERSISTENCE AND PERSEVERANCE

The ability for you to focus, stick to a task, face adversity along the way, and eventually persevere to will be the most biggest differentiator in your personal and business lives. If you can't take "no" for an answer and bounce back, or if you can't fail at a project and then bounce back for bigger and better things, you will be in for a disappointing and unrewarding life.

Conclusion

In the words of Renan, "Quand on a le droit de se tromper impunément, on est toujours sûr de réussir. " "If you are allowed to make mistakes, you are sure to succeed."

CAREER PATH EXAMPLE: BECOMING A GLOBAL MANAGER FOR STARTUPS, COMPANIES, & NGOs

"A word fitly spoken is like apples of gold in baskets of silver."
— PROVERBS 25:11

"I've been in this game for years, it's made me an animal, There are rules to this game, I wrote thee a manual, A step-by-step booklet for you to get, Your game on track, not your dreams pushed back."
— Celebrated American poet CHRISTOPHER G.L. WALLACE
(Slightly modified version of a verse from the album, "Life After Death")

People in the general management profession are in charge of the direction and control of a business or other enterprise, whether it be a small retail shop or a large manufacturing floor. Working with employees to set goals and expectations and helping achieve them is a major part of management. While they can have many different titles, these are all jobs of high responsibility, held by the people who are ultimately responsible for the success or failure of an organization.

THE GLOBAL MANAGER AND EXECUTIVE

In this new era managers will be faced with an array of challenges, and will have to balance being jacks-of-all-trade with mastery over many parts of the business. Simply put, you will need to know a lot about a lot to ward off threats to the business or to your position, and more importantly take advantage of opportunities for your business. Topnotch managers and executives who can achieve success in this new environment will be in high demand, and will be paid well.

WHY ADD A GLOBAL COMPONENT TO YOUR FUTURE MANAGERIAL EXPERIENCE?

It's not a requirement for success to add some overseas experience to your resume. However, the differentiation in global experience will give you an edge over competitors seeking the same positions, and the international experience or interest may be the characteristic that gets you in the door in the first place. According to the Harvard Business Review, "the more expats interact with locals and local institutions, the more creative and entrepreneurial they'll become." In other words, the more you can experience life overseas in your early years (before age 40), the more you can increase your ability to be creative, entrepreneurial, and resourceful. And that can all translate into success in the business world. So why not help them give it a shot if you have an opportunity?

In any case, here are the skills that future global managers will need:

<u>SOFT SKILLS</u>

- Ability to work with teams concurrently
- Ability to work with diverse groups of people
- Ability to identify talent and delegate tasks accordingly
- Ability to guide a group towards consensus
- Ability to conduct efficient meetings
- Ability to incorporate different perspectives into overall corporate strategy
- Superior negotiation skills
- Ability to truly observe and listen
- Ability to make quick decisions and to be decisive
- Ability to operate in a changing environment without all the desired information available
- EQ skills; knowing when to push staff, when to back off, and when to compromise is essential to a global manager's long-term success

<u>HARD SKILLS</u>

- Operations management skills
- Financial analysis skills
- Ability to read, understand, and question profit/loss and balance sheets

- Ability to calculate profits and margins, including with international business deals where hidden costs may not be spelled out
- Presentation skills

ADDITIONAL SKILLS THAT HELP INCLUDE:

- Sales skills: Managers that understand sales processes and the challenges salespeople face can work more effectively with their teams and command respect from front-line people.
- Legal skills: In this litigious society, knowledge of business law and legal considerations never hurts. From an international perspective, having more legal awareness may help to keep the company out of trouble or provide opportunities for the company to save costs and reduce risks
- Tax accounting skills: A basic understanding of international taxation issues will help you gain a quicker understanding of the financial situation

TYPICAL UNIVERSITY MAJORS

- Business administration
- Finance - Accounting
- Management
- Political science

ADDITIONAL RECOMMENDED COURSES

In addition to the courses you'll take for a major in one of the subjects above, if the courses below aren't requirements, you should consider taking them to round out the knowledge portfolio:

- Negotiation
- International negotiation
- International business
- International management
- Sales
- Strategy or strategic planning
- Conflict resolution

RECOMMENDED READING

- Crucial Conversations: Tools for Talking When Stakes Are High, by Kerry Patterson, Joseph Grenny, Ron McMillan and Al Switzler
- Getting to Yes: Negotiating Agreement without Giving in, by Roger Fisher and William Ury
- The Goal: A Process of Ongoing Improvement, by Eliyahu M. Goldratt and Jeff Cox

Recommended Study Aboard or Homestay Experience: **ASIA PACIFIC**

- Singapore
- Australia
- Taiwan
- Japan
- Vietnam
- South Korea

Recommended Languages to Study (IN NO SET ORDER):

- Mandarin Chinese
- Japanese
- Korean

Recommended Study Aboard or Homestay Experience: **LATIN AMERICA**

- Panama: This is one of the most dynamic countries in the world, with economic growth stemming from international trade, banking, manufacturing, casinos, and more.
- Mexico (violence and unrest notwithstanding)
- Brazil
- Argentina
- Colombia
- Costa Rica: It's the center for many manufacturing and technology facilities for multinational Latin American operations.

- Chile: This country is well-regarded for business and economic development.
- Miami: Many managing directors for Latin American entities operate out of Miami.
- Uruguay

Recommended Languages to Study (in this order):

- Spanish
- Portuguese

Recommended Study Aboard or Homestay Experience: **EUROPE**

- United Kingdom
- Spain
- France
- Germany/Austria
- Netherlands
- Belgium
- Denmark
- Switzerland

Recommended Languages to Study (in this order):

- German
- French
- Spanish
- Portuguese
- Italian

Managers and Executives Specializing in EMEA (EUROPE, MIDDLE EAST AND AFRICA) Markets

In addition to the recommended homestay or study abroad experience above for Europe, those interested in the EMEA experience may want to add these additions, time and health restrictions permitting:

- Turkey
- South Africa
- Dubai

- Abu Dhabi
- United Arab Emirates
- Ghana (there are successful Ghanaian businessmen around the world; we've done business with some in Japan)
- Jordan

RECOMMENDED LANGUAGES TO STUDY (IN THIS ORDER):

- Arabic
- French

CHAPTER 16

BLK ENTREPRENEURSHIP

Everyone needs a side hustle. Or a side company they can crank up to generate revenue, and create their own economy.

If you're making over $300,000 with your full-time, active job, then you're exempt from this rule IF you're saving at least 20% of your income every year, and you have guarantees that your job will continue for another 5 years.

Otherwise, you need to come up with a side hustle.

Questions:

- Did you know entrepreneurs can enjoy tax benefits including write-offs on automobiles, home offices, and more?
- What percentage of small businesses go out of business in the first year? In the first five years?
- How can you increase your chances of your side hustle or small business surviving?
- And who can you learn from along the way to increase or guarantee your chances of success?

Everyone can become an entrepreneur or create a side hustle. I am an accidental entrepreneur. I have been turned down for multiple jobs that I was well-qualified for by banks and by one Chamber of Commerce. And every time I got turned down, I was extremely disappointed and suffered short-term financial pain. But today I have to thank all of those groups that turned me down because they forced me to create my own path.

Entrepreneurship can be a lonely and tough road, but if you have a plan and persevere, it can be incredibly empowering and rewarding to grow your own business and become your own boss. People overestimate the value of high paying, low freedom positions. They underestimate the value of high freedom, medium paying businesses that can create passive or residual income, or both.

My company Insurance Advantage™ was started by accident. My brother had a question about health insurance for him and some guys at his bar. I told him I had no idea, but that I would do research on it and try to find someone who could help him. As I did research, I realized that it might be an opportunity for a business, and I ran into a guy at a networking event that worked in the employee benefits space. He introduced my brother and myself to a group that had health insurance expertise, and our business was born.

Even after the first 3 years, it was still a side hustle until a government policy change kicked into effect. Initially that government change actually eliminated our original business idea overnight. So we pivoted, grew slowly but surely, and then 3 years later, after lots of research, we decided to take turn the government policy on its head and become experts in it for the benefit of the underserved communities that we were serving.

Over the years, as we've looked at expansion opportunities that make sense after we become experts in our target market, we have gone into additional fields that are underserved by partnering with an expert in that new field to grow and expand the market. And we have expanded into fields that help and educate people for free all while creating passive and residual income streams for the firm.

The possibilities in terms of revenue and freedom are beyond your imagination for entrepreneurs. And the earning power and momentum typically build over time for companies that are set up properly.

So, what is your mission? Find out what you're great at, do it, improve it, and continue until you're an unstoppable force for good (and delivering value).

CHAPTER 17

FAMILY BUSINESS

Thousands of the wealthiest families in the United States (think about the Fords and the Waltons (of Walmart fame) have built and passed on family businesses (or family stock holdings) to not only their families but also to communities, non-profits, and universities they support.

The possibilities in terms of revenue and freedom are beyond your imagination for entrepreneurs. And the earning power and momentum typically build over time for companies that are set up properly.

Notable family businesses include:

- Walmart – The Waltons
- The Dallas Cowboys – Who has Jerry Jones appointed to management positions? His children.
- The Lakers – Who owns the Lakers? The Buss Family Trust, the family that has owned them since 1979.
- Tyson Chicken – Tyson is officially a publicly owned company, but the Tyson family still controls a large percentage of the company's shares.
- The Mars Family – They make candy bars, and have created a pet food empire. And are billionaires.
- The Ford Family – They started with cars, and now they own the Detroit Lions among other assets.

So, what is your mission? Find out what you're great at, do it, improve it, and continue until you're an unstoppable force for good (and delivering value). And along the way, consider using reliable, smart, hungry family members and friends to help you build your business and expand your mission.

Employing Your Children

(And legally reducing the overall Family Tax Bill)

Exercises for Entrepreneurship & Family Business Ideation

1. Pick 5 successful entrepreneurs to study (diverse sets ideally, so Jay-Z, the owners of Lidl, Jeff Bezos, Elon Musk, The Kardashians or Rihanna, The Waltons, Warren Buffett, or others); and write 2 sentences on how or why they have been successful

2. Listen to an entrepreneurial or side hustle podcast for 1 month (at least 5 episodes)

3. Listen to the "How I built this" podcast (at least 5 episodes)

4. Review the 10 most recent startups to go public on the NYSE or NASDAQ stock exchanges – Visit https://www.iposcoop.com/last-100-ipos/. List at least 3 sectors that these IPOs are in.

5. Pick 2 entrepreneur biographies to read or listen to.

6. Jot down at least 2 entrepreneurial ideas you have. Even if you never act on them it's good to put them down on paper.

CHAPTER 18

DIVIDEND INVESTING

What if, with relatively small amounts of money, you could become part owner of some of the world's most successful and best run companies?

And what if you could buy ownership in companies that actually paid you every year, quarter, or even month to be a part owner?

Lastly, what if you could buy enough ownership in the world's most successful companies that pay their owners to quit your job and retire?

This is the power of a dividend.

Uneducated or under-informed people think that studying wealth-building options like dividend investing are boring. Wealth builders know that dividend-producing stocks can be one of the keys to building wealth and controlling your own future. Dividends are sexy.

Specific benefits of buying dividend-producing stocks

- Passive Income: If you buy the right company's shares, you can hold that stock for decades and watch the dividends ($$$) roll in.
- Residual Income: Hundreds of companies pay dividends every year, quarter, or even month. And the income continues to come in as long as you hold the company's stock. So dividend investing can not only be passive but also residual. This is the holy grail of investing and wealth building.
- Inflation Hedge: Receiving dividends on a consistent basis can be one of the most effective ways to keep pace with inflation.
- Tax Savings: Income from dividends can be taxed at a lower rate than income from your active job or business.
- The Ultimate Boss Move: Buy enough dividend-producing stocks. Watch the $ roll in. And quit your job.

Bottom line: If you have enough dividends coming in you can quit your job and call your own shots. Don't believe me?

Ask Warren Buffett. His company receives $4.3 billion in dividends per year. Could you live off 1/100th of 1% of that ($4.3 million)? Not sure about you, but I know I could.

Building a diversified dividend-paying stock portfolio, and reinvesting those dividends, is a long-term wealth building strategy. In this chapter we're going to look at the definition, the deciding factors in which ones to purchase, how to purchase them, and a success story.

What exactly is a dividend and dividend-producing stock?

A dividend-producing stock is a share (your share or piece) of a company that regularly distributes a portion of its earnings to shareholders in the form of cash or additional stock.

Dividends are profits paid by that company to its shareholders. Typical publicly traded companies' dividends can range from 0.5% per year up to even 9% per year.

Some companies don't choose to distribute profits in the form of dividends to shareholders. They reinvest profits back into their organizations or buy back their stock (to potentially increase the price of the stock). And some companies just sit on the cash they collect.

Companies have the right to set their own dividend payout schedules. Many issue dividends annually or quarterly, and some even issue dividends on a monthly basis.

Interest in dividend stocks usually rises when the economy is in a low-interest rate environment where investors or retirees are making less by holding fixed-income assets. Over the last 20 years, interest has risen substantially in dividend stocks, especially as companies have started paying attention to dividend payouts, and as more ETFs, REITs, and MLPs have become available for purchase on the market. Share of personal income from dividends rose from 7.3% in the first quarter of 2022 from 3.2% in the first quarter of 1980.

*(S&P Dow Jones Indices and Bureau of Economic Analysis data)

How do you choose ones to invest in?

There are several metrics you can use to assess which dividend stocks to purchase. These metrics include underlying fundamentals like:

- Dividend yield
- Consecutive years of paying dividends
- Price-to-earnings ratios
- Dividend payout ratio – What is the percentage of dividends paid out vs. earnings per share? A range of 30% to 55% is typically considered healthy from an investor's point of view.
- Earnings per share – Does the company make enough profit per share (that you own) to pay you a dividend?
- Historical dividend payout data – Has the company consistently paid dividends over the last decade? Have the dividends been consistent, or better yet, has the dividend yield grown?
- Debt & the balance sheet – Is the company heavily indebted? How much of the earnings per share might they utilize to pay off debt?
- Sales growth estimates – Is the company growing or shrinking in terms of sales and profits?
- Recent news – Has the company had bad news in the last 2 years? You can research this via Yahoo Finance or other websites that track publicly traded stock news.

The best performers in terms dividend yield will typically have a great mix of many of these fundamentals above.

How can you shorten the list of potential dividend stocks to purchase?

Study and potentially copy top dividend investors – If you don't have to reinvent the wheel, why would you? There are hundreds (maybe thousands) of articles on top dividend investors like Warren Buffett, who has ranked anywhere from the #1 to #9 richest person in the world since 1991.

Study and potentially buy or emulate dividend ETFs – Want to reap the rewards of investing in dividends, but want to avoid the higher fees of mutual funds? One great option is to study ETFs that are designed to cash in on companies that distribute dividends.

How do you find these ETFs? You can literally search for "Dividend ETFs" and you'll find them. You can also go to Yahoo Finance (finance.yahoo.com), type in "dividend" in the ticker symbol box at the top, and you'll find plenty of dividend ETFs. Once you find them, you can look at their profile to see the top 10 stocks they've invested in. Or you can actually go to the ETF's actual website to see the entire portfolio of stocks they've invested in.

Or you could copy the "Dividend Aristocrat" lists. "Dividend Aristocrats" are typically large dividend-paying companies (stocks) that have solid income-generating businesses and have a history of raising their dividends every year over the last 20+ years. There is even an index, the S&P 500 Dividend Aristocrat Index, that you can study. Or copy at your discretion.

Some of the well-known dividend aristocrats include companies like IBM and Exxon Mobil.

What are common mistakes you can make when investing in dividend stocks?

The biggest mistake is searching for and then buying high dividend yielding stocks without taking underlying fundamentals into consideration. Some stocks have high dividend yields for good reasons, and some stocks have high dividend yields because their stock price has dropped or the management team is trying to extract cash for reasons that may be great for you or bad for you as an investor (shareholder).

What are the ways to invest in dividend stocks?

You can buy individual stocks, or you can buy dividend ETFs or mutual funds. ETFs and mutual funds provide diversification (the ability to spread your money around across several (sometimes hundreds of stocks and dozens of industries) instead of putting all your money in one investment.

Dividend ETFs typically have lower fees and better tax efficiency than many mutual funds, especially the actively managed mutual funds, so please do your own research (as always) to determine which individual stocks, ETFs, mutual funds, REITs, CEFs (closed-end funds), or MLPs (master limited partnerships) may be right for you and your hard-earned money.

Can you reinvest your dividends?

Yes, you can. And you should do it automatically if you can! This is a simple, consistent way to become an "automatic millionaire" over time.

Reinvesting dividends can allow you to outpace the broader stock market indexes, and this practice can allow you to take advantage of what Albert Einstein called the "8th wonder of the world", Compounding.

Dividends & Taxation

How dividends are taxed depends on whether they are classified as qualified or non-qualified. This distinction in classification can be based on IRS criteria including how long you are going to hold the stocks. Other factors include the type of account that holds your dividend-producing stocks (Roth IRAs, taxable accounts, etc.) and your taxable income.

Disclaimer: As with everything else in this book, you are an adult (or an intelligent pre-adult). Please consult with a licensed and trained professional in your jurisdiction for your specific situation.

Success Stories

Warren Buffett

Out of 7 billion people on the planet, Warren Buffett has been ranked in the top 10 in wealth worldwide since 1993 when he made his debut at #9 on the World Richest People list. The "Oracle of Omaha" has been ranked as high as #1, and he has not fallen out of the top 10 list since 1993. Did you hear that?!

Dude has been at on the Top 10 Richest People in the World list since 1993! Think Tom Brady, Serena Williams, or Michael Jordan are the GOATs (greatest of all time)? You're wrong. Warren Buffett is.

And how has he accomplished this amazing feat of building and sustaining massive wealth? Through dividends.

This, my friends, is the power of value investing, and more specifically, dividend investing.

For over 4 decades Warren Buffett has bought "boring" companies that produce dividends. This seemingly boring practice has developed into one of the world's largest companies and portfolios that now gets spits out $4+ billion a year, just in dividends.

Buffett's dividend portfolio has included:

- Bank of America
- Occidental Petroleum
- Citigroup
- Wells Fargo
- Verizon

Building Wealth Ideas

Be like Buffett. You can:

- Study his current portfolio (available publicly through Berkshire Hathaway's website or other websites)
- Study articles about his current and past portfolios and how he analyzed the stocks in them
- Study other financial and investment managers that copy Buffett

There are thousands (maybe hundreds of thousands) of smart investors that follow, copy, and emulate Buffett (copy then potentially come up with even better models).

Should you be one of them? Only you can decide that.

The Non-Billionaire Idea:

Besides copying or emulating successful dividend investors like Warren Buffett, you can also seek other opportunities through dividends.

One idea that I am currently putting in place is to buy shares of companies that I spend my money with. This includes companies like:

- Verizon
- Apple
- Target

My goal is to buy enough shares of each company to receive enough dividends to pay for anything I spend with the company. So, in other words, if my Verizon bill is $100 a month, I want to build a portfolio of Verizon stock that pays me $100 x 12 months = $1200 a year to cover my Verizon bill.

A View towards Retirement & Freedom

If you build up a $100,000 portfolio that pays out 5% a year in dividend stocks, that will produce $5,000 before taxes in income for you.

Now, what if you build a $500,000 or $1,000,000 dividend stock portfolio (keeping in mind that Warren Buffett has a $100 billion portfolio so you can do this!), that would produce $25,000 or up to $50,000 per year.

Could you retire on $50,000 a year? I know a lot of people who could. Once you start buying dividend producing stocks, ETFs, or other shares, you can

DIVIDEND TERMINOLOGY

Declaration date. The date a company announces it will be issuing a dividend in the future.

Ex-dividend date. The cutoff date on or after which purchasers of a stock won't receive the next dividend payment.

Record date. The date a company makes final the list of shareholders who are eligible to receive the dividend payment. If you invest in the company's shares after the record date, you won't receive that dividend payment.

Payment date. The day the company credits dividends to shareholder accounts.

Dividend growth rate. The annualized average rate of increase in the dividends paid by a company. Growth rates can be based on any interval.

Dividend per share. The company's total annual dividend payment divided by the total number of shares outstanding.

Dividend yield. A financial ratio that shows how much a company pays out in dividends each year relative to its share price.

Dividend payout ratio. The percentage of net income distributed to shareholders in the form of dividends.

ETF. An exchange traded fund which is composed of a basket of stocks and can be bought or sold just like a stock. ETFs sometimes have lower fees and greater tax efficiencies for investors than mutual funds have.

Total return. The gain or loss generated from a stock, based on its price change and dividend payments.

Qualified dividend. A dividend that is taxed at capital-gains tax rates, rather than ordinary income-tax rates, because it meets certain IRS criteria, including how long the investor has held the stock. Capital-gains rates are 0%, 15% or 20%, depending on an investor's income level.

Nonqualified dividend. A dividend that doesn't meet IRS criteria for capital-gains tax treatment and is thus taxed at the investor's ordinary income-tax rate, which can range from 10% to 37%, depending on income level.

Dividend rollover plan. A strategy in which an investor buys a dividend-paying stock shortly before its ex-dividend date and then sells shares after the dividend is paid, hoping to secure income.

Dividend reinvestment plan. A program that automatically uses the proceeds from dividend stocks to purchase more shares of the company.

*Sources: Investopedia, Corporate Finance Institute

TAKING ACTION

Action talks, and BS walks, right? Correct.

So, am I employing this strategy right now? Yes.

Do I wish I started this exact strategy 20 years ago, even when I was making less income? You damn skippy.

Here's a slice of the dividend action from my own portfolio over a 7-day period.

*Note: Returns and dividends may vary (of course).
This is simply a real snapshot from my portfolio. Do your own research.

CHAPTER 19
REAL ESTATE

Most Americans, and indeed most people around the world, build their largest sources of wealth and equity through the purchase and long-term holding of their home. In fact, according to Kiplinger, housing equity makes up about two-thirds of all wealth. So simply put, if you can purchase a reasonably priced home, or if you can afford to purchase even an expensive home in a desirable area that it a surefire bet to appreciate over time, then go for it.

How do you pick the best city or region to purchase real estate in? Please see Chapter 6 where we talk about How to Pick the Best City.

An additional consideration, regardless of politics, is the impact of potentially changing weather patterns, and the potential occurrence of natural disasters in the area you are looking to buy your primary home or other real estate.

Before you plop down hundreds of thousands of dollars or even millions for what may be your biggest purchase, I advise you to study the actual natural disaster (flood, hurricane, tornado, earthquake, fire) trends & information in the area you're looking to move to or invest in. Here are some practical (if not unusual but necessary) questions to ask yourself about the area or real estate in the area in general:

- Does it flood often?
- Can I purchase property at a higher elevation or in a non-flood zone?
- What is the likelihood of forest fires or soil erosion?
- How much have property & casualty insurance companies increased home insurance rates in the last 5 years? You may have to contact an insurance agency to get this data.
- How many insurance carriers have stopped providing coverage in the area, or how many have indicated they might?

- How many natural disasters have hit the neighborhood/city/state in the last 10 years?
- What type of structure should I buy (brick, reinforced steel, concrete, etc.)?
- What sort of roofing does it have? Can it withstand a hurricane, tornado, etc.?

Real Estate Investment: The Options

There are multiple types of ways that you can invest in real estate. They include:

- Longer-term rental properties
- Short-term rental properties (AirBNB, VRBO)
- Commercial real estate
- Financing
- REITs

Longer Term Rentals

When you get started analyzing the opportunities with long-term rental properties, it's important to understand the types that are available:

- Single family homes
- Multi-family properties including duplexes, triplexes, quadplexes, and apartment properties
- Condos

Before you purchase, you should review some of the same data from Chapter 6 on "How to pick a city".

Single family homes can be good investments depending on factors including where you buy, the demand for housing in that area, and the cost needed to renovate the property and get it on the market.

Multifamily real estate is intriguing and potentially lucrative due to the cost efficiencies that you can achieve by purchasing one property with multiple units that can:

- Be renovated all at the same time with the same crew
- Produce multiple revenue streams so that you aren't dependent on one tenant
- Have one insurance and tax bill that can be spread out over multiple tenants

And with multifamily property, once you get your "system" down, you can scale up by using the expertise you've gleaned and the revenue produced, along with the potential equity in your first property, to purchase more properties and grow a larger revenue stream.

Condominiums are interesting long-term investment properties to analyze, with some pros and cons.

Positives of Condos

Low external maintenance – Don't want to cut the grass, or fix the roof? A condo may be for you.

Shared services covered by HOA (the condo homeowners association or membership board) – Typically, condo HOA fees will cover trash pickup, recycling, and even your water bill.

Negatives of Condos

The HOA fee – It is a never-ending cost, you don't have full control over it (unless you own a majority of the condos in the association), and the fees typically go up each year or two.

The HOA board – Hopefully they aren't crazy or fiscally liberal with your hard-earned HOA fee. If they are, you may be in trouble.

Short-Term Rentals

In the last 10 years, the short-term rental market has exploded with the advent of AirBNB, VRBO, and other short-term rental market players. It's a huge industry that has shown no signs of slowing.

The good news is that single family homes, multifamily properties, and condos can all be used to produce short-term rental revenue.

To get your short-term rental business going, you should consider the following:

- Location, location, location.
- Management – Who's going to manage it?
- Current market for your area – What are the price or accommodations comparisons for units and properties in your area?
- Sustainability over the next 10 years – Is your town maintaining, coming up the curve, or looking more and more like a nuclear dumpster fire every day? Before you buy, you better know.
- Can you House Hack (see below)? Can you live in one part full-time and rent the other part of the house out on a short-term basis?

Commercial Real Estate

Whether it's an office building, a retail storefront, an old house (like my firm purchased), a dentist's office, or a restaurant, you can buy it, build it, or renovate it, and then use it for your business or put it on the market for rent.

The analysis to be done and the questions to answer before purchase are very similar to the ones for personal or rental property usage. Commercial properties, however, can be more complicated to analyze and come up with appropriate prices to purchase them.

Real Estate Revenue Generation Hacks

1. House hacking – You buy a house, condo, or multifamily property with several rooms or units, you live in one of the units or sections, and you rent out the rest to cover your mortgage & build your equity.

2. Geographic hacking – You buy a primary home, move to another city where you buy another home, and you rent out your 1st primary

home all while covering the mortgage for it and hopefully profiting. There are people that have built mini real estate empires by moving 3-4 times and repeating this process.

3. Geographic arbitrage – You can house hack, hack geographically across the U.S., and then move overseas to a country that is cheaper and experiencing less inflation so that you can live off of the cash flow from your properties.

CHAPTER 20

EMPLOYEE BENEFITS & INDIVIDUAL INSURANCE

Insurance typically sucks, unless you need to use it. Our motto at our independent insurance brokerage Insurance Advantage is that "We make insurance suck less".

Insurance is essentially a financial contract that provides coverage and compensation in the event of certain defined losses or risks. It acts as a shield against financial devastation due to unforeseen circumstances.

One of the most important decisions in your life (besides deciding where to live) is deciding on which employee benefits to take advantage of at your job. Whether you're an attorney, healthcare worker, bus driver, or even a property & casualty insurance agent (seriously), deciding on benefits for you and your family can be nerve-wracking and fraught with opportunity for big mistakes.

This chapter will make it much easier to decide on which benefits and how much of each benefit you need so that you'll be at peace with the process, and all set should something unexpected happen.

Quick Summary:

- Health Insurance: At the very least, take the high-deductible plan and sock money away in an HSA if possible. This prevents you from being in a position of financial disaster if you need the insurance and have no coverage. Having zero health insurance is like playing Russian Roulette.
- Dental and vision insurance: You may or may not need it, depending on your projected use during the year. But if it's "affordable" take it since you have no idea what may come up.
- Disability insurance: If you have less than $5,000 in the bank, take the short-term disability. If you have less than $5,000 in savings, take the long-term disability too. If your company doesn't offer it, call my team or someone to get it offered. You

very likely will not be able to get the insurance cheaper on your own.

- Life insurance: If you don't have anyone counting on you (i.e. spouse or kids), then make sure you have enough for your family to be able to bury you without having to come out of their pocket.

If you do have obligations (a spouse or children under the age of 18), you think you are an adult man or woman, and you don't have adequate life insurance (at least 5x your annual salary, or at least $250,000 if you are a homemaker), then you need to rethink your assumptions about you being an "adult". It is irresponsible and selfish to have people that you "love" depending on your income for their lifestyle and future prospects if you don't have any life insurance to support them should you die tomorrow. We see this happen all the time, and it's tragic. So unless you are over 65 years old, load up on the life insurance available through your job. If you can get some on your spouse via your job, it probably makes sense to load up on that too.

Seriously, if you have a spouse, kids, and/or a mortgage, **I'm talking to you. Don't stick your head in the sand**. Load up on the life insurance at 5x – 20x your annual salary at least. Once you're gone, or once your spouse is gone, it's too late.

Company insurance vs. Individual Insurance:

Typically speaking, you will not be able to find cheaper dental, vision, short-term disability, long-term disability, or life insurance (the group term life insurance) on the individual market. So particularly on the disability and life insurance, you should load up.

For health insurance, the answer is that it literally "All depends" on each individual and company scenario, so this is where you may need to consult with a professional.

However, if your company offers you as the employee (not your family) health insurance coverage that costs 9.5% or less (per current Affordable Care Act rules as of the time of publication), you will typically not be eligible to take advantage of subsidized health insurance on the Federal or state health insurance marketplaces. If your company offers you "affordable" coverage, but the coverage for your family does not seem "affordable", you can check with the Federal Marketplace at 1-800-318-2596 or consult with a professional health insurance agent to see if your family qualifies for the "family glitch" exemption that may allow them to take advantage of subsidized health insurance through the exchanges.

Health Insurance

If you don't have health insurance and something bad happens and you get a $100,000 or $1,000,000 bill for example, you're liable for that entire bill. If you have health insurance, your exposure is usually going to be capped at $6,000 - $10,000 maximum, depending on the plan you got. Uncapped medical bills are one of the largest drivers of bankruptcy in the United States. So at the very least you need to get a high-deductible policy and ideally combine that with an HSA account, which we discuss later on in this chapter.

Health Insurance Definitions

- Premium – the price of the insurance
- Deductible - The amount you pay for covered services before the plan starts to pay.
- Co-pay – The dollar amount you pay for a covered service after you meet your deductible
- Co-insurance - The percentage of cost you pay for a covered service after you meet your deductible.
- Maximum out of pocket (MOOP) - The most you'll have to pay for covered services in a year, no matter how much care you need. Once you spend this amount for covered services in a year, your plan pays 100% for your care.
- Health Savings Accounts (HSAs): A Health Savings Account (HSA) is a tax-advantaged account created for or by individuals covered under high deductible health plans (HDHPs) to save for

qualified medical expenses. Contributions are made into the account by the individual or their employer and are limited to a maximum amount each year.

• HRAs: A health reimbursement arrangement (HRA) is an employer-funded plan that reimburses employees for qualified medical expenses and sometimes insurance premiums as well.

• ICHRAs: With an ICHRA, businesses, nonprofits, churches, and other employers can reimburse employees tax-free for individual health insurance premiums and other medical expenses. ICHRAs can involve employees picking their own individual health insurance on the Federal Health Insurance Marketplace or state marketplaces.

Decision-Making Process

Generally speaking, people want the lowest premiums, deductibles, copays, coinsurance, and MOOPs possible. The problem is typically the lower the premium, the higher the deductibles and copays. So the goal is to find a happy medium i.e. a reasonable premium with reasonable deductibles and MOOPs, plus reasonable copays to go see primary doctors, specialists, get prescription drugs.

HSAs: The SuperHero in Your Health Insurance Benefits

If your job offers an HSA-component, then you should seriously consider taking advantage of the HSA. Why should you use HSAs? There are lots of reasons:

A Health Savings Account (HSA) offers several advantages that can make it a valuable tool for managing healthcare expenses and saving money. Here are some key reasons to consider using an HSA:

Tax Benefits

- Triple Tax Advantage: Contributions to an HSA are tax-deductible, earnings grow tax-free, and withdrawals for qualified medical expenses are also tax-free. This triple tax advantage is unique and maximizes your savings potential.

- Lowering Taxable Income: Contributions to an HSA reduce your taxable income, which can lower your overall tax bill for the year.

Long-Term Savings

- Investment Options: HSAs will often allow you to invest your funds in stocks, bonds, or mutual funds, which can substantially grow your savings over time. This is especially beneficial if you plan to use the funds for future healthcare costs or as a supplement to your retirement savings.
- No "Use-It-Or-Lose-It" Rule: Unlike Flexible Spending Accounts (FSAs), HSA funds roll over year to year, allowing you to build a substantial nest egg for future medical expenses. And you can even use these funds after you retire and become Medicare-eligible.

Flexibility

- Wide Range of Qualified Expenses: HSA funds can be used for a variety of medical expenses, including deductibles, copayments, prescription medications, and even some over-the-counter (OTC) drugs and medical supplies
- Portability: HSAs are not tied to your employer. If you change jobs or retire, your HSA goes with you, giving you continuous access to your savings.

Retirement Planning

- Supplementing Retirement Income: After age 65, you can use HSA funds for any purpose without a penalty (although non-medical withdrawals will be subject to income tax). This flexibility makes it a useful supplement to traditional retirement accounts.

- Medicare Premiums: HSA funds can be used to pay for Medicare premiums, which can be a significant expense in retirement.
- High-Deductible Health Plan (HDHP) Compatibility
- Encourages Cost-Conscious Healthcare Decisions: Since HSAs are paired with HDHPs, they encourage you to be more mindful of healthcare spending, potentially leading to more cost-effective healthcare decisions.
- Lower Premiums: HDHPs typically have lower premiums compared to traditional health insurance plans, which can save you money upfront.

Emergency Fund for Health Care

- Immediate Access: HSA funds can be used immediately for qualified medical expenses without the need for waiting periods or extensive paperwork, providing a reliable emergency fund for health-related costs.

Summary of HSAs:

By leveraging the tax advantages, flexibility, and investment opportunities provided by an HSA, you can effectively manage your healthcare costs and enhance your financial planning for both short-term needs and long-term goals.

Factors to Consider when getting Health Insurance

1. Budget – How much premium can you afford?
2. Usage – How much do you use health insurance? Any needs you know about coming up within the coverage year?
3. Copays – Do you go to specialists once or twice a month? Do you go to see specialists or doctors 4 times a month? Do you have a brand prescription drug that costs $100 (or $400) out of pocket? If so, you need to pick the plan that provides good copays.
4. Catastrophic Coverage – If you get a $7,000 bill this year, can you cover it out of pocket with no worries, or via your HAS? Or will

it cripple you financially, and you would prefer that the insurance company cover it?

5. Supplemental Coverage – Does your company offer supplemental coverages, or do you have supplemental benefits on your own like accident, critical illness, cancer, hospitalization, hospitalization gap, or other insurance?

Employee Benefits and Medicare-Eligibility

Yes, you can use Health Savings Account (HSA) funds with Medicare, but there are specific rules and considerations to keep in mind:

Using HSA Funds with Medicare

1. Eligible Expenses: Once you're enrolled in Medicare, you can use HSA funds to pay for qualified medical expenses, including:

- Medicare premiums (except Medigap premiums)
- Deductibles, copayments, and coinsurance for Medicare
- Prescription drugs
- Dental, vision, and hearing care
- Certain long-term care expenses

2. Medicare Premiums: Specifically, HSA funds can be used to pay premiums for:

- Medicare Part B (medical insurance)
- Medicare Part D (prescription drug coverage)
- Medicare Advantage (Part C) plans

3. Medigap Policies: HSA funds cannot be used to pay for Medigap (Medicare Supplement Insurance) premiums.

Contributions to HSA After Medicare Enrollment

- Eligibility to Contribute: Once you enroll in any part of Medicare, you can no longer contribute to your HSA. This includes enrollment in Medicare Part A or Part B. Contributions must stop the month your Medicare coverage begins.
- Enrollment Timing: It's important to plan your HSA contributions carefully around your Medicare enrollment. For example, if you turn 65 and sign up for Medicare, ensure you stop contributions to avoid tax penalties.

Using HSA Funds Without Penalty

- Age 65 and Older: After you turn 65, you can use HSA funds for non-medical expenses without the 20% penalty. However, these withdrawals will be subject to ordinary income tax.
- Qualified Medical Expenses: Withdrawals for qualified medical expenses remain tax-free, even after you enroll in Medicare.

Strategic Considerations

- Rollover and Accumulation: Before enrolling in Medicare, maximizing HSA contributions can be a strategic way to save for future healthcare expenses. The funds roll over year to year, allowing you to build a substantial balance.
- Healthcare Cost Planning: Using HSA funds for healthcare expenses in retirement can help preserve other retirement savings accounts, such as 401(k)s and IRAs, for non-healthcare expenses.

Summary

Using HSA funds with Medicare is an effective way to manage healthcare costs in retirement. However, it's crucial to understand the restrictions on contributions once you enroll in Medicare and to plan accordingly to maximize the benefits of your HSA. By leveraging HSA funds for eligible medical expenses, you can enjoy tax-free withdrawals and better manage your healthcare costs as you age.

Dental Insurance

Summary: Dental insurance can truly suck. The reason for the potential suckiness is that each dentist is different. Some of them accept multiple dental insurance company carriers. Some of them accept only 1. And some of them accept none. Also, sometimes the dentist will accept none, but will file your dental insurance anyway to see if there are any discounts or partial coverages that you can take advantage of.

If you want to just have your teeth cleaned, one more affordable option (that you can freely research on your own) that does not include dental insurance is to find a dental assistant school at a local community college or trade school where you can get your teeth cleaned by people in training.

For major orthodontic work, or for dentures, some dental insurances will cover this work, and some will not. So, once again, we encourage you to fully read what is available through dental coverage offered at your job. And then ask your dentist or orthodontist what will be covered if you use that insurance at their practice.

Dental Insurance Definitions

- PREMIUM – the price of the insurance
- DEDUCTIBLE - The amount you pay for covered services before the plan starts to pay.
- CO-PAY – The dollar amount you pay for a covered service after you meet your deductible
- CO-INSURANCE - The percentage of cost you pay for a covered service after you meet your deductible
- MAXIMUM - typically refers to the maximum amounts the dental insurance company will pay for you each year.

The DECISION-MAKING PROCESS:

Generally speaking, group dental plans are usually inexpensive. If you have to pay more than $35 per month as an individual for your plan, you're in a questionable group dental plan. Your company needs to shop it out, or renegotiate the terms with the current insurance carrier. Dental plans are great if you have major work coming up that you know about. If your employer dental plan is $25 or less, it probably makes sense to take it every time as long as you are taking advantage of your 2 cost-free cleanings every year.

If a major dental issue hits, you will want to have full dental coverage.

FACTORS TO CONSIDER

- BUDGET – How much premium can you afford?
- USAGE – How much do you use dental insurance? Any needs you know about that will be coming up in the next year?
- WAITING PERIODS – Does the plan have waiting periods for major dental work? If so, for how long?
- CATASTROPHIC COVERAGE – If you need a $4,000 oral surgery done, and you don't have dental coverage, are you up the creek without a paddle?

Vision Insurance

DECISION-MAKING PROCESS:

Generally speaking, group vision plans are going to be $15 per month or less. If you have to pay more than that, you really need to put down on paper how much the coverage will provide for you vs. how much you'd pay out of pocket for your expected use of vision doctors & providers within the year.

DISABILITY Insurance

(Aka your PAYCHECK PROTECTION)

"Ben, don't ever get your priorities confused. A man's first priority is the job. The 2nd is your family. And the 3rd is your church. Why? Because if you don't have a job, your family doesn't need you, and your church doesn't want you."

- My grandfather William Green

Why do you need disability insurance?

For men and women, that quote says it all. The most important thing you do financially is produce a paycheck. Disability insurance can cover you for 2 months, 2 years, 2 decades, or more (up to the age of 65).

According to The Social Security Administration, about one in four of today's 20-year-olds will become disabled before they reach age 67. This means a lot of loss of income, retirement plan contributions, and more.

If you can't go to work tomorrow, will that break you financially? Probably not.

But how about if you can't go to work for one month? Or 6 months or 12 months?

Do you have 6 months in savings? Do you have a year of expenses saved in your bank account? Or how about 5 years of expenses saved for in the bank account if you get into a bad accident?

A 2023 survey by the Federal Reserve found that about 36% of adults would have difficulty covering an unexpected $400 expense, suggesting that many do not have adequate emergency savings. If you need $3000 - $10,000 per month to pay the bills and make sure your family doesn't starve, and you don't have that type of money in the bank, then you may need not only short-term disability insurance but also long-term disability insurance.

And for high-income earners who have high fixed expenses (like $5000 mortgages or $35,000 private school bills), your company's standard Long-Term disability policy may not be nearly enough to cover your monthly expenses. In this instance, you will need additional supplemental long-term disability. Many doctors, dentists, and other physicians regularly carry high levels of disability insurance because of how financially crippling it would be if they could not go to work for 6 months, 6 years, or for the rest of their lives.

What Causes Disabilities?

According to the Council for Disability Awareness, the most common causes of long-term disability include:

- Musculoskeletal disorders (like back pain, arthritis)
- Cancer
- Heart & Cardiovascular diseases
- Injuries and
- Mental health issues

Disability Insurance Definitions

- DISABILITY INSURANCE – Provides income in the event that you can't work due to a disability. We call it paycheck protection since it protects your ability to earn a living. You can
- ELIMINATION PERIOD - Length of time that you have to wait after becoming disabled before you can receive benefits
- BENEFIT PERIOD – The amount of time you can receive the benefits for (3 months, 6 months, 1 year, 2 years, 5 years, 10 years, and up to age 65)
- SHORT-TERM DISABILITY - This coverage can kick in normally in as little as 14 days. They even have 7- day elimination periods. The payout varies, but is typically around 60% of your salary, for up to 3 months.
- LONG-TERM DISABILITY - This coverage can kick in after a 90 or 180-day elimination period. The payout varies, but is typically around 60% of your salary, for 6 months, 1 year, 2 years, or even to age 65, however long that is.

DECISION-MAKING PROCESS:

The bottom line is "How much money do you have" in the Generally speaking, group vision plans are going to be $15 per month or less. If you have to pay more than that, you really need to put down on paper how much the coverage will provide for you vs. how much you'd pay out of pocket for your expected use of vision doctors & providers within the 12 month calendar year.

LIFE INSURANCE

"Ben, don't ever get your priorities confused. Your first priority is your job. The 2nd is your family. And the 3rd is your church. Why? Because if you don't have a job, your family doesn't need you, and the church doesn't want you."

- My grandfather William Green

The same quote from the disability section is applicable here.

What is your most important asset?? You and your earning power of course. This is why sufficient life insurance coverage is critically important.

Imagine losing the ability to create an income for your family forever, not because you're disabled (which is more likely), but because you died.

If you die at the age of 99 like my Grandad did, by that time you have turned your Human Capital into Financial Capital. And in the financial sense, this is not a tragedy.

If you die at the age of 29, leaving behind a wife and 2 kids under the age of 10, like one of our former clients did, the potential 70-plus years that you could have had converting your Human Capital to Financial Capital is gone forever. And if that Human Capital was not accounted for through the use of a life insurance policy (at a rate of $1 million per $50,000 earned annually), then this is not only a great personal tragedy.

This is a HUGE FINANCIAL DISASTER for your family that they may never recover from.

- Depending on the financial situation, we have seen people lose:
- Houses
- Children's plans for college
- Retirement plans for their spouses
- Their entire comfortable lifestyle
- Life insurance on the job

Life Insurance Definitions

- PREMIUM – the price of the insurance
- TERM LIFE - Coverage for a specified term (10, 20, or 30 years), or until you are no longer employed
- WHOLE LIFE – Coverage that can last your entire lifetime
- UNIVERSAL LIFE - Universal life insurance is permanent life insurance with an investment savings portion and premiums that are usually lower than whole life insurance premiums.
- CASH-VALUE LIFE - usually referred to as whole life insurance, cash value life is a form of permanent life insurance that features a cash value savings component. You can use the cash value for many purposes, such as a source of loans or cash or to pay policy
- premiums.
- DEATH BENEFIT - the amount your beneficiaries will get in the event of your passing.
- BENEFICIARIES - the people, trusts, charities, etc. that you designate to receive funds in the event of your passing
- PAID UP - Paid-up additional insurance is additional whole life coverage that a policyholder purchases using the insurance policy's dividends instead of premiums.
- The paid-up portion allows you to increase your death benefit and living benefit by increasing the policy's cash value.
- GUARANTEED-ISSUE - This means that you can sign up for life insurance with no questions asked.

- Portable vs. non-portable: Most often, life insurance that is offered on the job via the group life insurance plan will not be portable, which means it can not be taken with you. This is sometimes different for the supplemental life insurance plans that are offered. And it is different for federal employees that have FEGLI (federal employees group life insurance) offered to them. Typically they can carry some of this life insurance with them into retirement. However, the premiums will continue to go up as they age, just like they do for the life insurance via the job.

DECISION-MAKING PROCESS:

Almost everyone needs life insurance. And generally speaking, up to the age of 55, your employer's group term life insurance plans will be really cheap. Generally speaking you should max out on what they have to offer, since it's usually cheap, and it's usually guaranteed issue. The maximum amount of term life insurance you can usually get is 2-3x your annual salary.

If you have no debt, no dependents, and no siblings or parents you want to leave money to if you die, then you need at least enough to bury you.

Otherwise, you probably need more. How much do you need? It all depends on your stage in life. Primary breadwinners can need up to 20x their annual salary for example, but even homemaking spouses during child raising years should be insured at $250,000 - $1,000,000 or more because of how valuable and irreplaceable their work is.

The equation that Tom Hegna (America's #1 expert on guaranteed income) advocates: For every $50,000 in income, you need $1 million in coverage. That might sound crazy until you think about a 30-year old with a wife, 2 kids, and a $500,000 mortgage passing away. That $1 million is going to get eaten up fast.

And let's think about the reverse. We insure a lot of couples where the woman is the primary breadwinner, sometimes bringing in 2-3x more than the man. If she is 35 years old and becomes permanently disabled or passes away, what is he going to do to replace that income???

The main question is: If you or your spouse/partner got hit by a bus tomorrow, will your family be fine? Or will they be begging for money on a GoFundMe campaign? Stay in control. Get fully insured.

FACTORS TO CONSIDER

BUDGET – How much premium can you afford?

DEBT/EXPENSES – How much do you owe on the house, cars, student loans, etc.?

DEPENDENTS – Does your spouse work? If so, what % of the income do they bring in? And how old are your kids? Do you have enough saved up to get them through primary school and college?

AGE – Do you have 30 more years ahead in your career, or are you retiring next year? Generally speaking, the younger you are, the more you need. But we have several clients in their 60's that are increasing their life insurance coverage through permanent policies.

SELF-INSURANCE OPTION – Unless you have at least $2,000,000 in the bank that your beneficiaries can have access to, "self-insuring" for life insurance is an idiotic idea. The way you need to think about it is this: If your surviving spouse is responsible, after taking care of some bills, they are not going to pull more than 5% from this $2 million bucket per year to fund their lifestyle. So, at that rate, that gives them $100,000 a year to cover their life. Is that enough? For some families, that is plenty. For many, just have $100,000 a year would plunge the family into poverty.

$1 million doesn't last as long as it used to, so taking advantage of a cheap term policy for $40 - $100 per month (depending on age, health) could be the most important thing you ever do for your family.

Summary:

You probably don't have enough life insurance. You need to fix that today.

SUPPLEMENTAL LIFE INSURANCE

Supplemental term life insurance policies are typically affordable. For whole life and universal life policies, you have to really review premiums to see if you could qualify for a cheaper individual plan. Up to 40% of Americans can't qualify for any life insurance outside of the job due to pre-existing conditions, weight, etc., so getting an individual life insurance policy may not be an option. And with universal life, you have to read the fine print, especially on what happens after you turn 70 or 75 years old.

FACTORS TO CONSIDER

- BUDGET – How much premium can you afford?
- Coverage needs – How much do you and your spouse/partner already have?
- Portability – Is the supplemental life insurance portable? And if you leave your job or get fired, how much life insurance will you take with you?

SUPPLEMENTAL INSURANCE

Supplemental coverage covers things like:

- ACCIDENTS – this type of coverage typically provides lump sum payouts for
- accidents; the payout can be tied to the severity of the accident
- CRITICAL ILLNESS (cancer, heart attack, stroke, etc.) – these plans can provide lump sums for major health events like cancer, heart attack, stroke, paralysis, etc.
- CANCER – These plans can cover out-of-pocket expenses like travel, hotel, food, etc. that are not covered, and are specifically designed for cancer.
- HOSPITALIZATION – plans that pay a set amount ($500 or $1000 per day for example) for every day you're in the hospital

- DEDUCTIBLES (gap plans) – plans designed to cover the deductible

DECISION-MAKING PROCESS

These supplemental coverages are all voluntary. If you have kids that are accident prone, if you have a history of cancer in your family, or if you have a huge family deductible that you can't pay if something bad happens, then you should consider these policies.

Supplemental Insurance Definitions

- VOLUNTARY – these supplemental /ancillary plans are usually voluntary; this means that you as an employee can pick and choose which ones you want to keep.
- PREMIUM – the price of the insurance
- DEDUCTIBLE - The amount you pay for covered services before the plan starts to pay.
- OUT-OF-POCKET EXPENSES – expenses like travel, hotel, food, etc. that are not covered.
- BUDGET – How much premium can you afford?
- SELF-INSURANCE OPTION TO COVER DEDUCTIBLES
- Do you have an HSA or savings to cover deductibles in the $1000 - $7,000 range? This is what it may take to satisfy your plans' deductible.
- OTHER EXPENSES – If you break your hands or legs and can't work for a month (even though your insurance covered the medical bills), will you be in financial trouble? If you get cancer and have to travel out of state for treatment, is your health insurance company going to cover those costs? Typically the answer is "no", and this is where supplemental plans like critical illness or cancer plans can come in handy.

LONG-TERM CARE INSURANCE

This is an issue that most Americans choose to act like 4-year olds about and stick their heads in the sand when the subject comes up, but because we're here to protect & preserve wealth, we're going to discuss it in this book.

People complain that LTC insurance is expensive. If you think $350 per month for 10 years is too expensive, imagine paying $150,000 a year for 3 years. Which one is more expensive?

Commonly confused with long-term disability coverage, long-term care coverage (LTC) provides nursing-home care, home-health care, and skilled nursing facility care for people that have need help with two of the 6 activities of daily living (ADLs).

Does Medicare or Medicaid cover LTC costs?

No. Medicare does not cover long-term care costs. It may cover a portion of a stay at a skilled nursing facility (typically 80% of that cost), but that is typically limited to 100 days per year.

Does Medicaid cover LTC costs?

Maybe. You or your loved one may qualify for Medicaid coverage in a long-term care facility or home health situation, but:

- You typically have to have very low assets & a lower income level
- The wait to get into a Medicaid facility may be really long (5 years or more). Florida and Maine for example have very long waits. Who is going to take care of you or your family member for the 5 years prior?
- When you pass away, the state may come after your remaining assets to recoup the cost.

So, you and your family may typically be on your own when it comes to covering the cost of LTC.

The impact of LTC costs on Wealth

LTC costs, quite simply, can destroy your retirement plans over time, and destroy large parts or all of the wealth of a family over time. So having a plan for it (that doesn't include sticking your head in the sand or telling your family to "Just put me outside in a field") is important.

Approximately 70% of today's 65-year-olds will require some form of long-term care during their remaining years. Women, in particular, are more likely to need long-term care due to their longer life expectancy and higher rates of chronic health conditions. On average, women need long-term care for about 3.7 years, compared to 2.2 years for men (Sources: SingleCare, Annuity.org, and the ACL Administration for Community Living).

The ADLs

The Long-Term Care Activities of Daily Living (LTC ADLs) refer to the basic tasks necessary for independent living. They are used to determine the level of care you or your spouse or loved one may require. The LTC ADLs typically include:

1. Bathing: The ability to wash oneself in a bathtub, shower, or by sponge bath.
2. Dressing: The ability to put on and take off clothes and any necessary braces, fasteners, or artificial limbs.
3. Transferring: The ability to move from a bed to a chair, wheelchair, or to stand up independently.
4. Toileting: The ability to get to and from the toilet, use it appropriately, and clean oneself.
5. Continence: The ability to control bladder and bowel functions.
6. Eating: The ability to feed oneself, not necessarily including meal preparation.

The other condition that is a usual trigger for LTC insurance to kick in is cognitive issues like dementia or Alzheimer's.

These activities are essential for daily self-care, and difficulty or inability to perform them can indicate the need for long-term care services.

If you can't perform them (for yourself or your spouse), who will, and how much will that cost? Glad you asked.

The Costs

The average cost of long-term care (LTC) varies depending on the type of care and the location. Here are the approximate national average costs for various types of LTC in the United States as of the year of publication:

1. Home Health Aide Services:
   - Hourly rate: $27
   - Monthly cost: $5,148
   - Annual cost: $61,776
2. Homemaker Services:
   - Hourly rate: $26
   - Monthly cost: $4,957
   - Annual cost: $59,488
3. Adult Day Health Care:
   - Daily rate: $78
   - Monthly cost: $1,690
   - Annual cost: $20,280
4. Assisted Living Facility:
   - Monthly cost: $4,500
   - Annual cost: $54,000
5. Nursing Home Care:
   - Semi-private room daily rate: $260
   - Semi-private room annual cost: $94,900
   - Private room daily rate: $297
   - Private room annual cost: $108,405.

* Sources: SingleCare, Annuity.org, and the ACL Administration for Community Living

These costs can vary widely based on geographic locations and the level of care needed for the person. People with dementia or Alzheimer's can cost more.

Long-Term Care Insurance Definitions

- REIMBURSEMENT – Typically refers to an LTC plan that reimburses the patient for expenses.
- INDEMNITY – Typically provides more freedom to decide where your money will go (i.e. you get sent the check, and then can decide where it goes)
- SELF-INSURANCE OPTION NOTES – Unless you have at least $1,000,000 in the bank just for long-term care costs, "self-insuring" for LTC can be a bad idea since it can blow up your retirement and leave you with $0 in assets. Even if you have $2 million in investments/savings, in a worst-case scenario (think Alzheimer's or dementia), your assets can be eaten up at a rate of $150,000 per year. If you're planning on leaving a legacy to your kids, grandkids, church, etc., then that can blow that plan out of the water. And many of the retirement accounts (401ks, 457s, 403(b)s, etc.) can be taxed heavily if you pass away, so "self-insuring" may be a bad idea for multiple reasons.

Key question: If you have $1 million in a retirement account and you're intelligent, why not peel $50,000 off the top to take care of this risk that is going to hit you 7 out of 10 times?

Indeed, we don't know why you wouldn't do that either.

RETIREMENT PLANS

Quick Summary:

For most employees that don't have a Roth component offered to them via their employer: You should consider contributing enough to get the full company match, and then from there, you should consider setting up a Roth IRA (or having a professional set one up for you).

For Federal employees or employees with organizations that have Roth components offered: Contribute what is needed to get the match, and then stuff the rest into the Roth component.

From there, you should look at other options that may keep you off of the radar of the IRS legally. These options do include Roth 401ks (if you own a business) and permanent cash value life insurance. Taxable brokerage accounts are also an option to consider, but once again, the gains and dividends may be taxable. So focusing on non-taxable and never taxable options going forward is key.

Why?

Why the need to fully consider where you put your retirement account money in going forward?

In three words, TAXES, DEMOGRAPHICS, and CONTROL.

Taxes

On the tax front, at the time of publication of this critically important book, the United States federal debt stands at $34.8 Trillion, which amounts to $104,000 in debt per citizen, but $267,000 in debt per federal taxpayer.

According to USdebtclock.org, by the year 2028 the U.S. national debt may stand at nearly $47 Trillion, or nearly $334,000 per federal taxpayer.

With the 2017 Trump tax cuts set to expire at the end of 2025, and with the United States federal tax rates at lows compared to World War II and other times when the federal government needed to drastically raise revenue, our country is likely at its very lowest federal tax point that we will see in the next 20 years.

With nearly $39 Trillion currently squirreled away in largely liquid & qualified (pre-tax) retirement accounts like 401ks, 457bs, 403bs, TSPs, and IRAs, where do you think the federal government will seek to get a large portion of revenue from to cover the debt and the interest on this debt?

In addition, many states in this country are facing structural, long-term deficits in their state budgets, and they will also be eyeing this nearly $39 Trillion worth of qualified retirement account assets to fill the budget holes. And based on the city you live in, even your city or municipality may come knocking on the door for a piece of your hard-earned 401k, TSP, or IRA since many of them are facing the same fiscal challenges that the states are facing.

Demographics

Many of you have heard these statistics, but now they are a reality. At the time of publication, every day, nearly 10,000 people are turning 65 years old in the United States. 2024 is actually the peak retirement year. While we applaud all of you that are retiring for all the hard work that you have put in, and while we are excited that many of you are finally able to hopefully enjoy your retirement, we also realize the following:

- Social Security used to be based on a 40:1 worker to retiree ratio; now it is closer to 3:1, and it was already strained
- This peak retirement phase will continue on for another 5-7 years at least
- Medicare is already strained, and the price of Medicare Part B may continue to go up due to this strain and due to inflation (was $15.50 in 1985, and is $174.70 in 2024)
- In addition to the U.S. official federal debt, based on the projection of all the people turning 65 and taking Social Security, the unfunded liabilities stand at:
- $27 Trillion for Social Security
- $41 Trillion for Medicare

How is the government going to pay for these programs? They will either:

- Cut benefits
- Raise the age requirements
- Provide means testing for the benefits
- Or raise taxes in other areas to fund this

There are literally no other options, unless you expect for the new Medicare and Social Security beneficiaries to vote against themselves and wind these programs down.

Control

Do you want to be in control, or do you want your tax situation to be outside of your control?

Perhaps the most compelling reason to implement the IRA Rescue Plan is so that you will have full control over your retirement savings.

And to get your retirement account silent partners (the U.S. federal government, your state government, and your local government) out of your business.

For every $1,000,000 in a qualified (pre-tax contribution) retirement account, you (the person that toiled away for 20-50 years for these assets) are typically only an 85% owner of the account, at best. Your "silent partners" in the deal typically own between 15 – 35% of the account.

You are typically the last stakeholder to get access to your funds, with the U.S. federal government, your state government, and even your municipal government stepping in line before you to take their 15-35% share of taxes before you get access to your money.

At the RMD (required minimum distribution) age, you are forced to pull money out of your account for the rest of your life.

And upon death, the "silent partners" truly back the Brinks truck up since your heirs have to officially draw down or liquidate and distribute the funds within a 10-year period, thanks to the SECURE Act. This 10-year rule can bring tax bills of 30%+, depending on who is inheriting the IRA and their tax status.

The Crystal Ball

As of the time of this writing, do you have any idea what the federal tax will be in the year 2030, 2040, or 2050 when you're looking to retire?

Contrast that complete lack of knowledge with where we know U.S. federal debt will likely be in the year 2028, 2029, and 2030. The year 2030 is likely when the rubber will fully meet the road and the U.S. government, just to service the debt payments, will likely be forced to:

1. Raise taxes drastically
2. Cut spending drastically

If you don't have Roth options through your job, look at them outside of the job.

Retirement Account Keys

The keys to maximizing retirement plans offered are:

1. MATCH: Maximizing the company match
2. TAXES: Taking full advantage of accounts that will provide you with tax-exempt earnings in the future (the Roth IRA)
3. FEES: Reducing fees within your mutual fund choices in the retirement plan system

Retirement Plans Definitions

- EMPLOYER MATCH – the amount your employer will contribute to your retirement plan
- MAXIMUM CONTRIBUTIONS – the maximum amount you can contribute to a retirement plan in a year
- TAX-QUALIFIED - A qualifying investment account means an investment purchased with pretax income. Funds used to purchase qualified investments are taxed when you make withdrawals from them.
- 401(K) PLAN – A 401(k) Plan is a defined-contribution retirement account that allows employees to save a portion of their salary, typically pre-tax. Penalty-free withdrawals start at age 59 ½, and will be taxable. 457 PLAN - 457 plans are tax-advantaged, deferred compensation retirement plans offered by state governments, local governments, and some nonprofit employers. You can make salary deferral contributions, depositing pre-tax money that is allowed to compound without being taxed until it is withdrawn.
- 403(B) PLAN - A 403(b) plan is a retirement account typically for employees of public schools and tax-exempt organizations

including teachers, school administrators, nurses, doctors, and professors.

- TSP - A thrift savings plan (TSP) is a type of retirement vehicle typically open only to federal employees, postal workers, and members of the armed forces or the reserves.
- IRA - An individual retirement account (IRA) is a tax-advantaged account
- that you can use to save and invest for retirement.
- SEP IRA - A simplified employee pension (SEP) is an IRA that your employer can set up. Your employer is gets a tax deduction for contributions made to a SEP IRA and makes contributions to each your plan on a discretionary basis.
- SIMPLE IRAS - A SIMPLE IRA is a retirement plan that many small businesses with 100 or fewer employees can use. Employers can choose to make a mandatory contribution of 2% of your salary or a dollar-for-dollar matching contribution of your contributions to the plan up to 3% of salary.
- ROTH IRAS - an individual retirement account that allows you to set aside after-tax income up to a maximum amount each year. Earnings on the account and withdrawals after age 59½ are tax-free.
- ROTH 401(K) - An employer-sponsored investment account funded with after-tax dollars up to the contribution limit. This type of account is may be good for people who think they will be in a higher tax bracket in retirement than they are now, or who think that taxes will be going up in the future, since withdrawals are tax-free.

DECISION-MAKING PROCESS:

If your employer offers a matching contribution, make sure you put enough into the account to capture the maximum contribution from your employer. Beyond that, you should consider Roth accounts within your employer platform or Roth IRAs, Roth 401ks, cash value life insurance, and brokerage accounts.

FACTORS TO CONSIDER

Discretionary income – How much is left over monthly after you pay the bills?

Retirement time horizon – Do you have 30 years before retirement, or 5 years? The

longer the run way, the smaller the amount you have to save.

Taxes – Due to the 2017 tax cut, we may be in the lowest tax environment of your lifetime. If that's the case, then the Roth IRA (where you pay taxes now on the "seeds" but don't pay taxes down the line on the "harvest" may be the best way to go).

Fees – How much does it cost (all costs and not just the stated costs) to invest in the funds offered through your employer's retirement plan? And if you maxed out your

Roth IRA contributions and put the rest of your discretionary income in index funds, would you match the market's performance while reducing the fees you pay?

Legal Notice (again): Of course, with all of these financial decisions, this book does not represent financial advice. Please consult a professional or do your own research before you make and implement these decisions.

STUDENT LOAN REPAYMENT Benefits

If your employer offers student loan repayment, this is typically a no brainer to accept since they're usually putting up all the money for the benefit.

MEDICARE-ELIGIBLE EMPLOYEES

If you are Medicare-eligible, here are some key FAQs (frequently asked questions) and considerations:

FAQ:

1. If I turn 65 and am still working for a company, do I need to apply for Medicare? Answer: It depends on the size of your company and if your company is offering a minimally essential policy. For those that work at companies of over 20 employees, assuming you have a health insurance policy with the company, you can apply for Medicare Part A (will typically be $0 for those that worked in a documented fashion for at least 10 years and paid into the federal system). Once you decide to fully retire, that is when you will apply for Medicare Part B and then look at either:
   a. Getting a supplement and Part D plan (or Medicare Advantage)
   b. Continuing your retiree health insurance plus the Medicare Part A & B coverage.

2. Will I be penalized if I don't apply for Part B when I turn 65? Answer: It all depends on your work situation. If you are working with an organization over 20 employees and you have health insurance through the organization, typically you will not need to apply for Part B, and you will not be penalized. If you aren't working, you may be penalized. Typically, even if you are retired & receiving retiree health benefits, you will need to apply for Part B once you turn 65 years old.

Considerations for Using HSA Funds with Medicare

1. Eligible Expenses: Once you're enrolled in Medicare, you can use HSA funds to pay for qualified medical expenses, including:

- Medicare premiums (except Medigap premiums)
- Deductibles, copayments, and coinsurance for Medicare
- Prescription drugs
- Dental, vision, and hearing care
- Certain long-term care expenses

2. Medicare Premiums: Specifically, HSA funds can be used to pay premiums for:

- Medicare Part B (medical insurance)
- Medicare Part D (prescription drug coverage)
- Medicare Advantage (Part C) plans

3. Medigap Policies: HSA funds cannot be used to pay for Medigap (Medicare Supplement Insurance) premiums.

Contributions to HSA After Medicare Enrollment

- Eligibility to Contribute: Once you enroll in any part of Medicare, you can no longer contribute to your HSA. This includes enrollment in Medicare Part A or Part B. Contributions must stop the month your Medicare coverage begins.
- Enrollment Timing: It's important to plan your HSA contributions carefully around your Medicare enrollment. For example, if you turn 65 and sign up for Medicare, ensure you stop contributions to avoid tax penalties.

Using HSA Funds Without Penalty

- Age 65 and Older: After you turn 65, you can use HSA funds for non-medical expenses without the 20% penalty. However, these withdrawals will be subject to ordinary income tax.
- Qualified Medical Expenses: Withdrawals for qualified medical expenses remain tax-free, even after you enroll in Medicare.

Strategic Considerations

- Rollover and Accumulation: Before enrolling in Medicare, maximizing HSA contributions can be a strategic way to save for future healthcare expenses. The funds roll over year to year, allowing you to build a substantial balance.

- Healthcare Cost Planning: Using HSA funds for healthcare expenses in retirement can help preserve other retirement savings accounts, such as 401(k)s and IRAs, for non-healthcare expenses.

CHAPTER 21

PROPERTY & CASUALTY INSURANCE

In the journey to building and preserving BLK wealth, one crucial aspect that also gets overlooked is the importance of property & casualty insurance.

Depending on the state, 50% of drivers don't have any auto insurance. And over 15% of homeowners don't have any homeowners' insurance (source: Insurify & ComfyLiving). Insurance serves as a safety net, offering protection and financial security for individuals and families in times of unexpected events. In this chapter, we're going to discuss the basics of property & casualty insurance, and what types you may need to protect yourself and your possessions.

Personal note: I am an insurance expert. And yet, I don't even DIY my own Property & Casualty policies. I rely on 2-3 P&C insurance agents that are experts in their field to confirm the coverages I need and then negotiate the price and secure the coverages for myself and my family's possessions. I encourage you to do the same since there are so many parts of P&C coverage that you can get wrong if you try to do it all yourself.

The Definitions

- Premium: The amount you pay regularly to maintain your insurance coverage.
- Policy: The document that outlines the terms and conditions of your insurance agreement.
- Coverage limits: A coverage limit is the maximum amount that an insurance policy will pay for a covered loss. It represents the cap or the highest dollar amount the insurer will pay under a policy for a particular type of loss or claim. Coverage limits are specified in the insurance policy and can apply to various types of coverage within the policy, such as:

▸Per Occurrence Limit: This is the maximum amount the insurer will pay for a single claim or incident. For example, if you have a homeowners' policy with a $400,000 per occurrence limit and you suffer a loss that costs $450,000 to repair, the insurance will pay up to $400,000, and you will be responsible for the remaining $50,000.

▸Aggregate Limit: This is the maximum amount the insurer will pay for all claims during a policy period which is usually one year. For instance, if your policy has a $1,000,000 aggregate limit and you have multiple claims totaling $1,200,000 during the policy period, the insurer will only pay up to $1,000,000, and you will have to cover the remaining $200,000.

▸Specific Limits: Some policies have specific limits for different types of coverage within the policy. For example, a homeowners insurance policy might have a $500,000 limit for the dwelling, $50,000 for personal property, and $10,000 for additional living expenses.

The Importance of Coverage Limits

1. Adequate Protection: Choosing appropriate coverage limits ensures that you are adequately protected in the event of a significant loss. Underinsuring can lead to substantial out-of-pocket expenses.
2. Premium Costs: Higher coverage limits typically result in higher premium costs. It is important to balance the need for adequate coverage with the cost of the insurance.
3. Legal Requirements: Some coverage limits are mandated by law, particularly in auto insurance. It is essential to comply with these minimum requirements.

Understanding coverage limits helps policyholders ensure they have sufficient protection for potential risks while managing insurance costs effectively.

Most Likely P&C Insurances Needed

Auto Insurance

If you own a vehicle, auto insurance is typically mandatory. It covers damages to your vehicle and liability for injuries or property damage caused by accidents. Shopping around for the best rates is essential.

Homeowners Insurance

Homeowners insurance protects your home and possessions from damage or theft.

Renters Insurance

Renters insurance covers your belongings if you're renting a property.

Umbrella Insurance

Umbrella insurance is a type of liability insurance that provides additional coverage beyond the limits of your existing policies, such as homeowners, auto, or boat insurance. It acts as a supplemental policy that kicks in when the liability limits of your standard insurance policies are exhausted.

Key Features of Umbrella Insurance:

1. Excess Liability Coverage: It provides an extra layer of protection for claims that exceed the coverage limits of your primary insurance policies. For example, if you are found liable for an accident that results in damages or injuries costing more than your auto insurance policy limit, umbrella insurance can cover the excess amount.
2. Broader Coverage: Umbrella insurance often covers claims that may not be included in your primary policies, such as libel, slander, defamation, and false arrest.
3. High Limits: Umbrella policies typically offer high coverage limits, starting at $1 million and can go up to $10 million or more.
4. Cost-Effective: Despite providing extensive coverage, umbrella insurance is generally affordable, especially when compared to the potential financial risk of large liability claims.

5. Worldwide Coverage: Many umbrella policies provide coverage for incidents that occur outside the United States, offering global protection.

Requirements:

To purchase an umbrella insurance policy, you typically need to have certain minimum liability coverage on your primary policies. For instance, your auto insurance might need a minimum of $250,000 per person/$500,000 per accident for bodily injury and $100,000 for property damage.

*Sources: Investopedia.com, Insurance Information Institute, The Balance.com

Umbrella insurance is an essential safety net that can protect you from significant financial loss due to unforeseen liability claims.

Why might you need $15 million in umbrella insurance protection?

As an example, you might be a famous athlete, and you might have been in an altercation in high school that has now resulted in an $11 million settlement that is going to force you to file for bankruptcy. Umbrella insurance could have potentially covered this.

CHAPTER 22

MEDICARE

Compliance Statement

Before we get started, Medicare is a highly-regulated area. We are not soliciting for Medicare business and solely seek to provide education in this chapter. Accordingly, per federal CMS (Center for Medicaid & Medicare) guidelines, we must state the following: "We do not offer every plan available in your area. Currently, we represent different numbers of organizations which may offer different numbers of products in your particular area, depending on which city and state you live in. Please contact Medicare.gov, 1-800-MEDICARE (TTY users call 1-877-486-2048) 24 hours a day/7 days a week, or your local State Health Insurance Program (SHIP) to get information on all of your options."

And good luck with all that (this is our quote).

Other disclaimer: These numbers below are all subject, just like everything else in this book, to change. That's why you need to do your own due diligence or speak with a licensed, knowledgeable person in your jurisdiction, on all topics in this book. These numbers and the information below for this chapter is based on the United States government, CMS, and other federal agencies.

Summary

Medicare is a critical component of healthcare in the United States, particularly for seniors and those with certain disabilities. There are important parts regarding Medicare that all Americans should understand and or be able to access knowledgeable advisors for their expertise in the field. They include:

- Understanding Medicare basics
- Understanding how to effectively utilize Medicare

- Understanding IRMAA (income-related Medicare adjustment amount) and how to avoid or appeal IRMAA "adjustments" when applicable
- How to select Medicare supplement, prescription drug, and Medicare Advantage plans
- What to do about dental, vision, and hearing coverage during retirement
- Understanding what Medicare does not cover
- Understanding how Medicare fits into your retirement & wealth preservation plans

Basics of Medicare (the partial alphabet)

Medicare is a federal health insurance program primarily for people aged 65 and older, but also for some younger people with disabilities or specific conditions. It is divided into four parts:

- Part A (Hospital Insurance): Covers inpatient hospital stays, care in a skilled nursing facility, hospice care, and some home health care. It typically covers 80% of the above coverage.
- Part B (Medical Insurance): Covers certain doctors' services, outpatient care, medical supplies, and preventive services. It typically covers 80% of the aforementioned coverage.
- Part C (Medicare Advantage): An alternative to Original Medicare (Parts A and B) that allows beneficiaries to enroll in private health plans that may offer additional benefits.
- Part D (Prescription Drug Coverage): Helps cover the cost of prescription drugs.

Enrollment and Costs

Automatic Enrollment: Most people are automatically enrolled in Part A and Part B when they turn 65 if they are receiving Social Security benefits.

Costs: While Part A is usually premium-free if you or your spouse paid Medicare taxes for over 10 years or 40 quarters of qualified work,

Part B requires a monthly premium unless you are Medicaid or extra help eligible.

In 1985, the Medicare Part B premium was $15.50 per month.

As of the time of this publication, it is now $174.70 per month and will be going to $185 per month in 2025. $15 x 12 = $180.

Has your income increased by a factor of 12 in the last 40 years? How about your investments, or your assets?

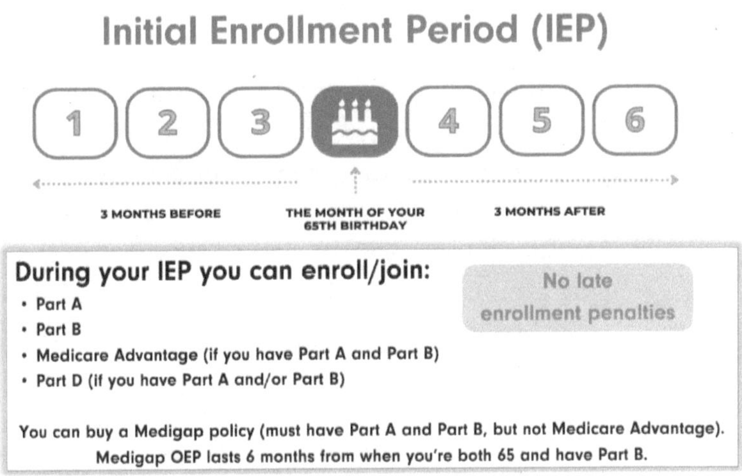

How to Qualify for Medicare

You need 40 credits (approximately 10 years of "above the table" work) to qualify for $0 premium (in layman's terms, "Free") Medicare Part A coverage. If you do not hit this requirement, your Medicare Part A coverage may cost between $270 - $510 per month (as of the publication of this document).

Understanding How to Effectively Use Medicare

In summary, if you get the basic Medicare A & B plus the Medicare supplement and Part D choices correct, you can greatly reduce and in fact, you can control your healthcare expenses in retirement.

If you get this process wrong, you can have an unlimited amount of healthcare cost exposure.

FAQ:

1. What if I have state, federal, military (Tricare or VA Care), union, or other coverage that I can take into retirement? Typically speaking, you will need to apply for only Medicare Part A and Medicare Part B, and not for any supplements, Medicare Advantage, or Part D prescription plans.

2. If I turn 65 and don't have access to any retiree health insurance (per above), what do I need to do? You will need to typically:
    - Apply for Medicare Part A & B ideally 3 months before you turn 65. Once you get the Medicare card with the specific effective date on it, you will need to either apply for a Medicare Supplement plan plus a Medicare Part D prescription drug plan -OR- you will need to apply for a Medicare Part C (aka Medicare Advantage) plan with prescription drug coverage.

3. What is the difference between Medicare Supplements and Medicare Advantage plans? Medicare supplements, also known as Medigap plans, can cover up to almost all of the other 20% of the coverage that Medicare Part A & B do not cover, depending on the plan that you select. Medicare Advantage plans typically have co-pays, deductibles, and maximum out of pockets that are usually higher than Medicare Supplement plans, but the premiums may be lower. Once again, to fully understand the differences you have several options (per the CMS guidance above) or you can consult with an advisor that is licensed in your state.

4. What is the highest level of Medicare supplement plan available? For those that are turning 65 this year and beyond, the highest level of Medicare Supplement plan is a Plan G.

5. Does it ever make sense to only have original Medicare Part A & B? Sometimes, but only in very specific circumstances, including if you are going into a nursing home. The question is always going to be: "Who is going to pick up the other 20% that Medicare A & B do not cover, and who or what will cover your prescription drug costs?"

6. If I have Medicare and Medicaid, what should I do? If this is the case, you may be eligible for special programs or plans, depending on your area. You should consult Medicare.gov, 1-800-Medicare, or you can talk with a licensed advisor that works in this field and understands what they are doing.

7. If I have VA-only care, what should I do? Once you become Medicare-eligible, typically you should get Medicare Part A & B, and then consult with Medicare.gov, 1-800-Medicare, or a licensed advisor that works in this field who may be able to tell you about additional programs or plans you are eligible for.

8. If I miss my initial enrollment period for Medicare supplement plans or wait for 10 years until I want to apply for them, will I be accepted on a guaranteed basis? No. You will be underwritten by the company (companies), and they will decide to accept you or reject you based on your health conditions.

Understanding IRMAA

IRMAA is a "surcharge" aka penalty that people with income above a certain amount must pay in addition to their Medicare Part B and Part D premiums.

The Social Security Administration (SSA) determines who pays an IRMAA based on the income reported on tax returns 2 years prior. So, for 2024, the SSA looks at your 2022 tax returns to see if you must pay an IRMAA.

IRMAA is calculated every year. That means if your income is higher or lower year after year, your IRMAA status can change. If the SSA determines you must pay an IRMAA, you'll receive a notice with the new premium amount and the reason for their determination.

Single	Married Filing Jointly	Married Filing Separately	Part B Premium	Part D IRMAA
$103,000 or less	$206,000 or less	$103,000 or less	$174.70	$0 + your plan premium
$103,000 up to $129,000	$206,000 up to $258,000	N/A	$244.60	$12.90 + your plan premium
$129,000 up to $161,000	$258,000 up to $322,000	N/A	$349.40	$33.30 + your plan premium
$161,000 up to $193,000	$322,000 up to $386,000	N/A	$454.20	$53.80 + your plan premium
$193,000 and less than $500,000	$386,000 and less than $750,000	$103,000 and less than $397,000	$559.00	$74.20 + your plan premium
$500,000 or	$750,000 and	$397,000 or	$594.00	$81.00 + your

Can I appeal the IRMAA?

Yes. You will need to fill out Form SSA-44 and tell them what your updated income will be.

Which plans to select?

Here is how Medicare works with Medicare Supplement, Part D, and Part C (Medicare Advantage) plans. You have 4 options.

1. Stick entirely with Medicare A & B only.
2. Stick with Medicare A & B plus Part D (prescription drug plan).
3. Add a Medicare supplement and Part D plan to the original Medicare (A & B).

4. Combine Part A & B into what's called Part C (Medicare Advantage) with plans that typically also include Part D coverage plus dental, vision, and sometimes hearing benefits (but not insurance).

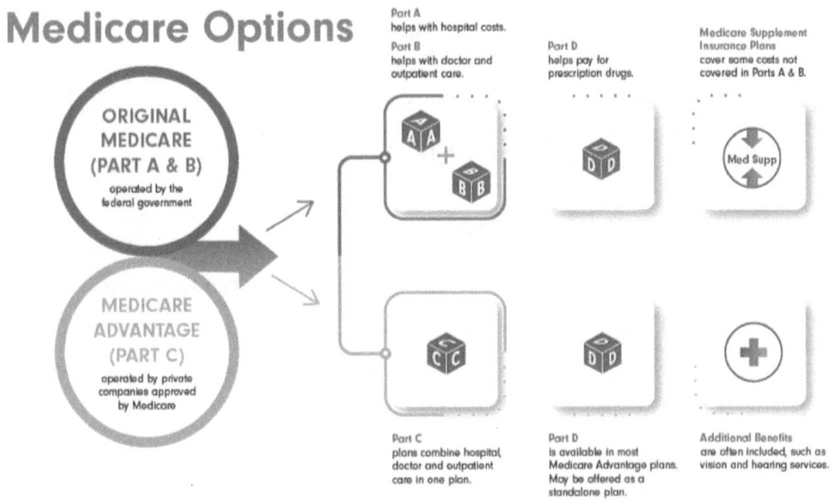

How to Select Medicare Supplement Plans

Selecting a Medicare supplement plan should be straightforward and simple. However, we have seen even super intelligent retired engineers, among others, choose to "DIY" it on their own and completely screw up the process and selection, with extremely detrimental consequences down the line once they are locked into the plans. All Medicare Supplement plans of the same letter have the exact same coverage. The difference lies in the:

- The price of the coverage
- The pricing history and trajectory of the private insurance company
- Size of the private insurance company
- The customer service experience of that company

How to Select Prescription Drug Plans

Medicare.gov typically does make it easy to select the appropriate prescription drug plan. You simply can go to Medicare.gov, put in your zip code, put in your prescriptions (you have to be exact on what you put in), and put in your pharmacy, and it will give you the top potential Part D plans.

How to Select Medicare Advantage Plans

Picking the correct Medicare Advantage plan can be as much "art" as it is "science", just like selecting the right retirement plan. If you want to do it all on your own, knock yourself out, but you were warned. The selection process can depend on a number of factors including:

- The networks and providers that the plan covers
- The referrals that may be required if the plan is an HMO (health maintenance organization) plan vs. a PPO (preferred provider organization) plan
- The copays
- The deductibles
- The MOOP (maximum out of pocket) on an annual basis for the plan
- The pharmacies that accept the PD (prescription drug plan) part of the Medicare Advantage plan
- The customer service experience of the plan
- The prior authorizations that may be required
- The premiums

Notice that we did not mention premiums first. With many MAPD (Medicare Advantage plans with prescription drug) plans, the premium might be $0 (plus the Medicare Part B premium that is necessary to qualify for the Medicare Advantage plan).

If you want to go on Medicare.gov or call the 1-800-Medicare number or your local state health insurance option and sift through dozens or hundreds of plans to select the right one, be our guest. Knock yourself out.

As my Grandad said, "Hard heads make for soft behinds".

Tip: Don't put your name and number on the Internet asking for Medicare information. You may get 30 calls per day regarding Medicare. Here's what to do if you need dental, vision, and hearing coverage:

If you want dental, vision, or hearing coverage, typically you will need to call these types of companies directly, or you need to engage the services of a licensed insurance broker that specializes in this area. Hearing coverage, in particular, can be difficult to find on its own.

If you used a licensed, knowledgeable broker to assist you with Medicare enrollment and Medicare supplement, PDP (prescription drug plan), or MAPD enrollment, then this person will probably be able to help you out with dental, vision, and hearing coverage as well.

Medicare.gov does not offer this coverage as of the time of this writing.

Understanding what Medicare does not cover

Long-Term Care is NOT covered by Medicare. And it may only be covered by Medicaid if you are potentially broke.

Some of the additional items and services that Part A and Part B DON'T cover include:

- Most dental care
- Eye examinations related to prescribing glasses
- Dentures
- Cosmetic surgery
- Massage therapy
- Routine physical exams
- Acupuncture or other types of acupuncture (like dry needling) for any condition other than chronic low back pain
- Hearing aids and exams for fitting them

• Concierge care (also called concierge medicine, retainer-based medicine, boutique medicine, platinum practice, or direct care)

They may be covered if you have other coverage, like Medicaid or a Medicare Advantage Plan that covers these services.

Understanding how Medicare fits into your retirement & wealth preservation plans

Simply put, just like everything else in the United States, if you screw up on the selection of these plans, it can have big financial ramifications for one year, or for the rest of your life and retirement.

If you get this process correct, it can severely limit your healthcare cost exposure and save you hundreds of thousands of dollars over your lifetime.

Conclusion

Medicare plays a crucial role in supporting the health and financial stability of Black Americans. By understanding the different parts of Medicare, the enrollment process, and the costs involved, individuals can better navigate the system to maximize their benefits. Proactive planning and utilization of available resources are key to preserving wealth and ensuring long-term financial health.

Further Reading and Resources:

- [Medicare.gov](https://www.medicare.gov)
- [National Council on Aging (NCOA)](https://www.ncoa.org)

CHAPTER 23

SOCIAL SECURITY

Currently, Social Security, which is in effect a guaranteed, lifetime annuity, is arguably the most vital component of financial stability and retirement planning for millions of Americans and specifically for millions of Black Americans. In fact, according to the SSA (Social Security Administration), it is estimated that 33% of Black Americans rely on Social Security for all of their income.

Understanding, optimizing, and effectively utilizing Social Security benefits is essential for building and preserving wealth. This overview provides key information on how Social Security can be leveraged to support long-term financial health and retirement income.

Basics of Social Security

Social Security is a federal program that provides financial benefits to retirees, disabled individuals, and survivors of deceased workers. It is primarily funded through payroll taxes collected under the Federal Insurance Contributions Act (FICA).

The Different Types of Social Security benefits

Retirement Benefits: Retirement benefits are based on your lifetime earnings and the age at which you start receiving benefits. Full retirement age (FRA) varies, but you can start as early as age 62 (with reduced benefits) or delay until 70 (for increased benefits). After age 70, the benefits do not increase with the exception of the COLA (cost of living adjustment), so at 70 years old the benefits are maxed out and you need to take the benefits unless there is some compelling tax reason not to.

Disability Benefits: For individuals who cannot work due to a qualifying disability. After 24 months of disability benefits, the beneficiary will typically also receive a Medicare card.

Survivor Benefits: These are benefits for spouses, children, and dependents of deceased workers:

- **Surviving spouse**

A surviving spouse who has reached full retirement age receives 100% of the deceased's benefit. If they are between 60 and full retirement age, they receive 71.5–99%. A disabled surviving spouse between the ages of 50 and 59 receives 71.5%, and any surviving spouse caring for a child under 16 receives 75%. Divorced spouses who qualify may receive the same percentages as widows and widowers.

- **Dependent child**

A dependent child of the deceased receives 75% of the deceased's benefit. This also applies to children who are 19 or younger and still in elementary or secondary school, or who have a disability.

- **Dependent parent**

A dependent parent of the deceased who is 62 or older receives benefits. One parent receives 82.5%, and two parents each receive 75%

*Source: SSA.gov, Investopedia

Social Security's Impact on Wealth Building

Social Security has several factors that make it so important to retirement plans over a 20 – 35+ year period.

These factors include:

- **Guaranteed Income**: Social Security is the world's most famous inflation-adjusted, lifetime annuity. It provides a stable source of income in retirement, reducing the risk of poverty and starvation, and enabling better financial planning for the long-term.
- **Cost-of-Living Adjustments** (COLA): Benefits are adjusted annually to keep pace with inflation, helping maintain purchasing power over time.

Progressive Benefits: The benefit formula is progressive, meaning lower-income workers receive a higher percentage of their pre-retirement income compared to higher-income workers.

Challenges, Opportunities, & Considerations for Black Americans Related to Social Security Optimization

Longevity and Health Disparities: Black Americans have historically had shorter life expectancies and higher rates of disability. While these factors can impact the total amount of benefits received, Social Security's disability and survivor benefits are critical for providing financial support, and currently provide all of the financial support available for 33% of Black Americans.

If you are 60 years old and have serious health issues or chronic conditions, it may not be appropriate for you to wait until you are 70 years old to claim your Social Security benefits.

On the other hand, if you are in excellent shape, can work until you are 68 years old, have $30,000 in expenses per year, and currently have only $100,000 in retirement savings, we may advise you to utilize your savings for 2 years while we let your Social Security max out at age 70 years old, and then you can claim your Social Security for the highest possible level of income from it that will last for the rest of your life.

Economic Disparities: Lower lifetime earnings and tougher paths to more well-paid employment can negatively impact the amount of Social Security benefits you receive.

Depending on the Social Security estimates, this will make it more imperative that you save as much as possible through retirement accounts like 401(k)s, TSPs, Roth IRAs, and more.

Spousal and Survivor Benefits: Ensuring that spouses and children understand their eligibility for benefits can be critical to maintaining financial stability and support.

Inflation & The COLA (cost of living adjustment) for Social Security

Plainly put, according to many sources, and our own internal estimates, the COLA adjustment that Social Security beneficiaries receive has not been keeping up with the true pace of inflation since at least 2010. In fact, according to this study, retirees' Social Security checks may have lost up to 20% of their purchasing power since 2010. So this is a major problem for ALL Americans when it comes to preserving wealth in retirement.

Social Security Optimization Strategies

Maximizing Benefits: Delaying benefits until age 70 can significantly increase monthly payments. Those who can afford to wait should consider this strategy.

Earning Credits: You need 40 credits (approximately 10 years of work) to qualify for retirement benefits. Ensuring continuous employment can help meet this requirement. If you don't hit this minimum level of activity, you will also likely not qualify for Medicare Part A (the $0 premium part of Medicare) as well.

Supplementing Income: While Social Security is crucial, it should be viewed as part of a broader retirement plan that includes savings, investments, and possibly a pension.

Social Security Taxation

Social Security income can be subject to federal income tax, depending on your overall income level. Here's how it works:

1. Combined Income Calculation: The IRS uses a figure called "combined income" to determine if your Social Security benefits are taxable. Combined income is calculated as follows:

- Adjusted Gross Income (AGI)
- Non-taxable interest (such as interest from municipal bonds)
- 50% of your Social Security benefits

2. Taxation Thresholds:

Single Filers:

- If your combined income is between $25,000 and $34,000, up to 50% of your Social Security benefits may be taxable.
- If your combined income is more than $34,000, up to 85% of your Social Security benefits may be taxable.

Married Filing Jointly:

- If your combined income is between $32,000 and $44,000, up to 50% of your Social Security benefits may be taxable.
- If your combined income is more than $44,000, up to 85% of your Social Security benefits may be taxable.

Strategies to Reduce Taxes on Social Security Income

1. Manage & Withdraw Funds Other Income Sources:

- Withdraw from Roth IRAs: Distributions from Roth IRAs are tax-free and do not count towards your AGI or combined income, helping keep your combined income lower.
- Limit Withdrawals from Traditional Retirement Accounts: Carefully plan withdrawals from traditional IRAs and 401(k)s to stay below the thresholds. You can stay below certain income thresholds that trigger Social Security taxation, and you can also stay below certain taxation thresholds to stay in the 12% bracket as opposed to the 22% bracket for example. See 2024 Tax Chart below for reference (only accurate as of 2024):

Single

Taxable income	Tax rate
$0-$11,600	**10%** of taxable income
$11,601-$47,150	$1,160 plus **12%** of the excess over $11,600
$47,151-$100,525	$5,426 plus **22%** of the excess over $47,150
$100,526-$191,950	$17,168.50 plus **24%** of the excess over $100,525
$191,951-$243,725	$39,110.50 plus **32%** of the excess over $191,950
$243,726-$609,350	$55,678.50 plus **35%** of the excess over $243,725
$609,351+	$183,647.25 plus **37%** of the excess over $609,350

Married filing jointly or qualifying widow(er)

Taxable income	Tax rate
$0-$23,200	**10%** of taxable income
$23,201-$94,300	$2,320 plus **12%** of the excess over $23,200
$94,301-$201,050	$10,852 plus **22%** of the excess over $94,300
$201,051-$383,900	$34,337 plus **24%** of the excess over $201,050
$383,901-$487,450	$78,221 plus **32%** of the excess over $383,900
$487,451-$731,200	$111,357 plus **35%** of the excess over $487,450
$731,201+	$196,669.50 plus **37%** of the excess over $731,200

Head of household

Taxable income	Tax rate
$0-$16,550	**10%** of taxable income
$16,551-$63,100	$1,655 plus **12%** of the excess over $16,550
$63,101-$100,500	$7,241 plus **22%** of the excess over $63,100
$100,501-$191,950	$15,469 plus **24%** of the excess over $100,500
$191,951-$243,700	$37,417 plus **32%** of the excess over $191,950
$243,701-$609,350	$53,977 plus **35%** of the excess over $243,700
$609,351+	$181,954.50 plus **37%** of the excess over $609,350

Standard deductions

<table>
<tr><th colspan="2">Filing status</th><th>Standard deduction</th></tr>
<tr><td colspan="2">Single/married filing separately</td><td>$14,600</td></tr>
<tr><td colspan="2">Married filing jointly</td><td>$29,200</td></tr>
<tr><td colspan="2">Head of household</td><td>$21,900</td></tr>
<tr><td rowspan="2">Additional (age 65/older, or blind)</td><td>Single, not surviving spouse</td><td>$1,950</td></tr>
<tr><td>Married filing jointly</td><td>$1,550</td></tr>
</table>

2. Tax-Efficient Investments for Consideration:

• Municipal Bonds: Income from municipal bonds is usually tax-free and can be used to generate income without increasing your combined income.

• Tax-Efficient Funds: Use tax-efficient mutual funds and ETFs to minimize taxable distributions.

3. Timing of Income:

• Delay Social Security Benefits: By delaying Social Security benefits, you can potentially reduce your combined income during years when you have other substantial income sources. Also, benefits increase each year you delay past your full retirement age up to age 70.

• Strategic Withdrawal Planning: Plan withdrawals from retirement accounts and other income sources strategically, spreading them over several years to avoid high combined income in any single year.

4. Adjust Living Expenses:

• Utilize Savings and Non-Taxable Sources: Cover living expenses with savings or non-taxable sources of income (e.g., Roth IRA distributions) to minimize taxable income. You can do this for a few years until you finish getting income from other areas.

5. Tax Deductions and Credits:

• Medical Expense Deductions: If you have high medical expenses, itemizing deductions may help lower your taxable income.

• Charitable Contributions: Making charitable contributions can reduce your taxable income through itemized deductions.

An Example Scenario:

Let's consider a married couple filing jointly:

- Adjusted Gross Income (AGI): $25,000
- Non-taxable Interest: $2,000
- Social Security Benefits: $20,000

Combined Income Calculation:

Combined Income} = $25,000 + $2,000 + (0.5 \times \$20,000) = $37,000

Since their combined income is $37,000, up to 50% of their Social Security benefits may be taxable.

Taxable Social Security Benefits:

By implementing strategies like reducing AGI through Roth IRA withdrawals or managing other income sources, they could potentially keep their combined income below $32,000, reducing or eliminating the taxation on their Social Security benefits.

Educational Resources and Assistance

Conclusion

Social Security plays a pivotal role in the financial security of Black Americans. By understanding the system, maximizing benefits, and incorporating Social Security into a broader financial strategy, individuals can significantly enhance their financial stability and wealth preservation. Proactive education and planning are essential to leverage Social Security effectively, ensuring a more secure and prosperous future.

Further Reading and Resources:

(a) Social Security Administration: https://www.ssa.gov

(b) AARP Social Security Resource Center (https://www.aarp.org/retirement/social-security/)

(c) National Urban League (https://nul.org/program/social-security-public-policy)

How can you optimize your Social Security?

Optimizing your Social Security benefits requires strategic planning and a good understanding of the rules and options available. Deciding when to take your Social Security can depend on dozens of factors including:

- Your retirement account savings
- Your non-taxable retirement account savings
- Your age
- Your health & longevity outlook
- Your spouse's income
- Your taxable income

Here are several strategies to help maximize your Social Security:

1. Delay Benefits if Possible

- Full Retirement Age (FRA): Your FRA depends on your birth year, typically between 66 and 67. Claiming benefits before your FRA results in reduced monthly benefits.
- Delayed Retirement Credits: For each year you delay claiming Social Security beyond your FRA, your benefits increase by approximately 8% until age 70. This can significantly enhance your lifetime benefits.

2. Maximize Your Earnings

- Work (in a system where you pay Social Security taxes) for at Least 35 Years: Social Security benefits are calculated based on your highest 35 years of earnings. Working fewer years can result in lower benefits because zeros are included in the calculation for the missing years.
- Increase Earnings: Higher lifetime earnings result in higher benefits. Strategies to increase your earnings include seeking promotions, changing jobs for higher salaries, or working overtime.

3. Coordinate with Your Spouse

• Spousal Benefits: If you are married, you can claim spousal benefits, which can be up to 50% of your spouse's benefit at their FRA. Coordinating the timing of each spouse's claims can maximize household benefits.

• Survivor Benefits: If your spouse passes away, you can claim survivor benefits, which can be up to 100% of your spouse's benefit. Planning to ensure the higher-earning spouse delays benefits can increase the survivor benefit.

4. Consider Health and Longevity

• Life Expectancy: If you have a family history of longevity or are in good health, delaying benefits may make more sense. Conversely, if you have health issues, it might be beneficial to claim earlier.

• Break-Even Analysis: This involves calculating the age at which the total benefits received from delaying exceed the total benefits received from claiming early. Tools and calculators are available online to help with this analysis.

5. Understand Tax Implications

• Taxation of Benefits: Up to 85% of your Social Security benefits may be taxable if your income exceeds certain thresholds. Understanding and planning for these thresholds can help minimize taxes on your benefits.

• Income Strategies: Managing other sources of retirement income, such as withdrawals from retirement accounts, can help keep your taxable income below the thresholds.

6. Use Retirement Income Planning Tools

• Social Security Calculators: Tools like the SSA's Retirement Estimator, AARP's Social Security Benefits Calculator, and financial planning software can help you evaluate different claiming strategies.

• Professional Advice: Consulting a financial advisor who specializes in retirement planning can provide personalized advice based on your specific financial situation and goals.

By employing these strategies, you can optimize your Social Security benefits and enhance your financial security in retirement.

By integrating Social Security into financial planning, Black Americans can protect their income, support their families, and build lasting wealth.

CHAPTER 24

LONG-TERM CARE COSTS & CONSIDERATIONS

Since LTC costs (both in $$ and in time spent) can completely destroy your family's wealth and health (for the caregivers), and since:

- Many Americans totally ignore this eventuality that up to 70% of us will face;
- And many "financial advisors" totally ignore this issue or tell their clients not to worry about this issue.

We're going to cover this issue twice in the book (for those of you that read about it in the Employee Benefits & Individual Insurance chapter).

Some of y'all who are reading this book are going to ignore this important part of your financial plan and literally rob your children and grandkids of their wealth, happiness, and even health. How is this possible? Across the United States grown children are quitting their jobs, delaying their career growth, and losing the opportunity to save money for retirement because they have to go take care of their parents. Regarding health, many long-term caregivers die before the people they are caring for die due to the emotional and physical stress. How might you rob your grandkids? Every dollar spent on LTC costs is a dollar that is not being passed on to the next generation.

Facing Reality & Preparing For It

This is an issue that most Americans choose to act like 4-year olds about and stick their heads in the sand when the subject comes up, but since we're here to protect and preserve wealth, we're going to discuss it.

"It's too expensive"

People complain that LTC insurance is expensive. If you think $350 per month for 10 years ($42,000) is too expensive, imagine paying

$150,000 a year for 3 years (i.e. $450,000). Which one is more expensive?

From personal experience, the LTC insurance premiums we would have paid for my father would have totaled about $10,000. Over the 2 years of care, the cost was $100,000. How is that for the math?

LTC is not LTD (long-term disability)

Commonly confused with long-term disability coverage, long-term care coverage (LTC) provides nursing-home care, home-health care, and skilled nursing facility care for people that have need help with two of the 6 activities of daily living (ADLs).

Does Medicare or Medicaid cover LTC costs?

No. Medicare does not cover long-term care costs. It may cover a portion of a stay at a skilled nursing facility (typically 80% of that cost), but that is typically limited to 100 days per year.

Does Medicaid cover LTC costs?

Maybe. You or your loved one may qualify for Medicaid coverage in a long-term care facility or home health situation, but:

1. You typically have to have very low assets and a lower income level
2. The wait to get into a Medicaid facility may be really long (5 years or more). Florida and Maine for example have very long waits. Who is going to take care of you or your family member for the 5 years prior?
3. When you pass away, the state may come after your remaining assets to recoup the cost.

So, you and your family may typically be on your own when it comes to covering the cost of LTC.

The impact of LTC costs on Wealth

LTC costs, quite simply, can destroy your retirement plans over time, and destroy large parts or all of the wealth of a family over time. So having a plan for it (that doesn't include sticking your head in the sand or telling your family to "Just put me outside in a field") is important.

Likelihood of Needing LTC care

Approximately 70% of today's 65-year-olds will require some form of long-term care during their remaining years. Women, in particular, are more likely to need long-term care due to their longer life expectancy and higher rates of chronic health conditions. On average, women need long-term care for about 3.7 years, compared to 2.2 years for men (Sources: SingleCare, Annuity.org, and the ACL Administration for Community Living).

The ADLs

The Long-Term Care Activities of Daily Living (LTC ADLs) refer to the basic tasks necessary for independent living. They are used to determine the level of care you or your spouse or loved one may require. The LTC ADLs typically include:

1. Bathing: The ability to wash oneself in a bathtub, shower, or by sponge bath.
2. Dressing: The ability to put on and take off clothes and any necessary braces, fasteners, or artificial limbs.
3. Transferring: The ability to move from a bed to a chair, wheelchair, or to stand up independently.
4. Toileting: The ability to get to and from the toilet, use it appropriately, and clean oneself.
5. Continence: The ability to control bladder and bowel functions.
6. Eating: The ability to feed oneself, not necessarily including meal preparation.

The other condition that is a usual trigger for LTC insurance to kick in is cognitive issues like dementia or Alzheimer's.

These activities are essential for daily self-care, and difficulty or inability to perform them can indicate the need for long-term care services.

If you can't perform them (for yourself or your spouse), who will, and how much will that cost? Glad you asked.

<u>The Costs</u>

The average cost of long-term care (LTC) varies depending on the type of care and the location. Here are the approximate national average costs for various types of LTC in the United States as of the year of publication:

1. Home Health Aide Services:
   - Hourly rate: $27
   - Monthly cost: $5,148
   - Annual cost: $61,776

2. Homemaker Services:
   - Hourly rate: $26
   - Monthly cost: $4,957
   - Annual cost: $59,488

3. Adult Day Health Care:
   - Daily rate: $78
   - Monthly cost: $1,690
   - Annual cost: $20,280

4. Assisted Living Facility:
   - Monthly cost: $4,500
   - Annual cost: $54,000

5. Nursing Home Care:
   - Semi-private room daily rate: $260
   - Semi-private room annual cost: $94,900
   - Private room daily rate: $297
   - Private room annual cost: $108,405

*Sources: SingleCare, Annuity.org, and the ACL Administration for Community Living

These costs can vary widely based on geographic locations and the level of care needed for the person. People with dementia or Alzheimer's can cost more.

How to pick a plan

Please consult with a long-term care insurance specialist or a life insurance specialist that has access to permanent life insurance policies that can include either:

- Long-Term Care riders
- Chronic care riders that trigger payments and use of the living benefits based off of the 6 ADLs plus cognitive issues like dementia and Alzheimer's

Generally speaking we like LTC plans or hybrid LTC/life insurance coverage options that have the following characteristics:

- Indemnity: Allow for indemnity payouts rather than having to reimburse the provider or the nursing home
- Paid up options: Will be paid up after a certain amount of time (like a 7-year, 10-year, or 12-year pay up option). This way, you don't have to pay for the rest of your life.
- Flexibility: offer several options for care including home health care, skilled nursing facility care, and nursing home care. The policies even allow for the insured to pay a relative to care for them.
- Return of Premium or a Death Benefit to go to a Beneficiary: No longer do you have to "use it" or "lose it". Many of the modern options now allow for the premium or even a large death benefit to go to the beneficiaries if you die and never need long-term care.

Are these options expensive? Not really, compared to the real cost of "self-insuring". From my personal family example, we would have paid out $15,000 in premiums for LTC. Instead, our family member (who refused to get LTC insurance coverage) paid out over $100,000 care costs to the facility.

What was more expensive? And was that an intelligent use of money?

SELF-INSURANCE OPTION NOTES – Unless you have at least $1,000,000 in the bank just for long-term care costs, "self-insuring" for LTC can be a bad idea since it can blow up your retirement and leave you with $0 in assets. Even if you have $2 million in investments/savings, in a worst-case scenario (think Alzheimer's or dementia), your assets can be eaten up at a rate of $150,000 per year. If you're planning on leaving a legacy to your kids, grandkids, church, etc., then that can blow that plan out of the water. And many of the retirement accounts (401ks, 457s, 403(b)s, etc.) can be taxed heavily if you pass away, so "self-insuring" may be a bad idea for multiple reasons.

Key question: If you have $1 million in a retirement account and you're intelligent, why not peel $50,000 off the top to take care of this risk that is going to hit you 7 out of 10 times?

Indeed, we don't know why you wouldn't do that either.

CHAPTER 25

ANNUITIES

"The first rule of investment is don't lose. The second rule of investment is don't forget the first rule." – Warren Buffett, the world's most successful investor for the last 40 years

Everyone and their mama has an opinion on annuities. Most of the opinions are outdated, totally inaccurate, or both. If someone says "I hate annuities", then they have no idea what they're talking about since the following are forms of annuities:

- Social Security payments
- Federal Employee Retirement (FERS) pensions
- State pensions
- County pensions
- Military pensions
- Firefighter pensions
- Police pensions
- Union pensions

Need we go on? If you "hate" annuities, please notify us and we'll tell you where you can send your monthly checks. Seriously. Otherwise, tell them to stuff it until they read this chapter and gain more education on an exceptionally important tool for many American's retirements.

At the max, only 2% of Americans fully understand annuities. Worst yet, only 5% of financial "advisors" and TV "experts" fully understand annuities at best. Why?

Because there are over 30 different types of annuities, there are over 200 different indices you can utilize within certain annuities, and there are over 80 annuity companies to choose from. Just like the **7000**+ mutual funds options, there are terrible annuities, there are mediocre annuities, and there are a few that are wealth building, wealth preserving, and retirement game changers. If you could identify the game changers, would you want that information? Intelligent people who want to build wealth and retire successfully certainly do.

History & Background

Annuities have been around for over 2000 years. They can be complex, simple, confusing, or exceptionally valuable. As part of an overall wealth preservation strategy, it's critically important to understand their uses or work with licensed, well-versed experts that understand their advantages, disadvantages, and how or when they can best fit into a wealth building & preservation strategy.

A Brief History of Annuities

The concept of annuities has a long and storied history, dating back to ancient times. The evolution of annuities can be traced through several key periods, each contributing to the development of these financial products as we know them today.

Ancient Origins

The earliest form of annuities can be found in ancient Rome over 2000 years ago. The Roman Empire utilized a system known as "annua," from which the modern term "annuity" is derived. This system involved making regular payments in exchange for a lump sum, often used to fund public works or provide for retired soldiers. Roman citizens could purchase life annuities, which guaranteed income for life in return for an initial investment.

Medieval Europe

During the Middle Ages, annuities continued to evolve. In the 14th century, the issuance of annuities became more structured, particularly in the form of what became known as tontines. Named after Lorenzo de Tonti, an Italian banker, tontines were a type of annuity that pooled investments from multiple individuals. Payments were made to surviving members, with the last survivor receiving the remaining funds. This system gained popularity in Europe as a way to raise funds for governments and municipalities.

Annuities in the 17th and 18th Centuries

The modern concept of annuities began to take shape in the 17th and 18th centuries. In 1693, the British government issued its first life annuity, primarily to fund the Nine Years' War against France. This initiative laid the groundwork for more sophisticated financial instruments. In 1774, the Society for Equitable Assurances on Lives and Survivorships was founded in London, marking the birth of modern life insurance and annuity products.

Annuities in the 19th and 20th Centuries

The 19th century saw significant advancements in actuarial science, allowing for more accurate life expectancy calculations and pricing of annuities. This period also witnessed the expansion of annuity products across Europe and North America. In the United States, annuities became increasingly popular in the late 19th and early 20th centuries, particularly as a means of providing retirement income.

Social Security – The World's Most Popular Inflation-Adjusted Annuity

The Social Security Act of 1935 further cemented the role of annuities in retirement planning. By providing a government-sponsored annuity program, Social Security highlighted the importance of guaranteed income for retirees. The mid-20th century saw the introduction of variable annuities, which allowed investors to allocate funds to various investment options, offering the potential for higher returns.

Annuity Innovation in the last 50 years

In recent decades, annuities have continued to evolve, offering a range of options to meet diverse financial needs. The introduction of indexed annuities in the 1990s provided a new way for individuals to participate in market gains while enjoying up to 100% protection against losses. Innovations such as living benefits and riders have enhanced the flexibility and appeal of annuities.

Today, annuities are a fundamental component of retirement planning for many individuals, offering various options tailored to different risk tolerances and financial goals. Income annuities are a testament to the enduring appeal of guaranteed income, a concept that has been refined over 2000+ years to adapt to changing individual retirement needs. In summary, if implemented and utilized correctly, annuities can provide three things that almost everyone wants:

- Predictability
- Guaranteed principal protection
- Guaranteed income for life

<u>Taxation, Liquidity, Caps, Participation Rates,Withdrawals, & Timeframes</u>

To tackle the typical questions first, we:

- Move assets from qualified accounts or non-qualified accounts over into annuities in a tax-free fashion
- Never put more than 60% of a client's $$ in an annuity unless they have robust, permanent cash flow already or a large emergency savings
- Seek to place clients in annuities and indexes with the highest interest rates, caps, and participation rates possible
- Seek to put clients in annuity solutions that have a 5-10% free annual withdrawal rate after the first year
- Rarely put clients in products that last over 10 years; the average timeframe is 6 – 10 years

<u>Who are annuities issued by</u>?

Annuities are issued by life insurance companies, which are typically regulated by all 50 states (or each state in which they do business).

The financial strength of life insurance companies is largely measured by their ability to meet long-term policyholder obligations, which is reflected in their reserves, investment portfolio, solvency ratios, and credit ratings.

Life insurance companies typically maintain a high asset-to-liability ratio to ensure they can meet their long-term obligations to policyholders. While the specific ratio can vary depending on the company and regulatory environment, a common target for many life insurance companies is to maintain an asset-to-liability ratio of around 1.05 to 1.15. This means that for every dollar of liability, the company holds between $1.05 and $1.15 in assets.

By comparison, banks generally maintain an asset-to-liability ratio around 1.02 to 1.05.

We typically don't work with companies that have less than a $1.10 to 1 ratio.

"I've been told that annuities suck."

If you think that annuities are great, guess what? You are right. They are great. If you have been told that they are great, guess what? The people that told you this are correct.

However, if you think annuities suck, or if you've been told they suck, guess what? This may also be correct. Like stock mutual funds, bond mutual funds, and "target date" or "lifetime" target date funds, probably 85% of them do suck, if you look at the:

- Fees
- Performance
- The caps on your performance

That's why we, as independent fiduciaries who run an independent insurance, retirement planning, and wealth preservation practice, eliminate 99.5% of the annuities we have access to when we are looking at the ones that are going to provide our clients with the best solutions. In fact, based on the data and experience we have, we often use the best-in-class solutions that have been nominated for awards. The annuities that our team recommends include the following characteristics:

- Low or zero fees
- Immediate or 12-month liquidity to fund your lifestyle
- The highest cap rates and participation rates possible in the industry
- Clear, transparent ties to benchmark indexes
- Guarantees

So, we're not here to argue with your Momma, Daddy, cousins, your hair salon stylist, or popular TV and radio hosts about annuities. Unless they have spent thousands of hours studying annuities -AND- have access to over 500 different annuities and indexes -AND- have access to software or reports to analyze annuity indexes, performance, and fees, there is no argument to be had.

We choose to utilize the top annuity solutions in the world for our clients. You can also choose to have access to these solutions. Or not.

Why do we use the top annuity solutions? Just like any other financial tool including 401ks, life insurance, and CDs, if used in an expert, intelligent fashion, annuities can:

- Guarantee financial harmony
- Guarantee that you don't run out of money in retirement
- Guarantee that you can sleep well at night
- Guarantee that you have a paycheck coming every month you live on this planet

Besides, popular income annuities (contracts between an individual and an organization that guarantee a monthly income stream) include:

- Social Security
- FERS – federal employee retirement system pension
- Military pensions
- School district pensions
- County government pensions
- State government pensions

If you aren't going to accept your Social Security payments, or you think that hardworking people should not use any of these guaranteed income streams as part of their wealth building and wealth preservation strategy, you can stop here and skip to the next chapter.

If you are going to use one of these strategies to build and preserve your wealth, continue reading and we'll fully educate you on the modern world of annuities.

Just recently (as in the last 6 months), 2 of America's largest asset management firms have jumped on the bandwagon and are now educating individual clients and employers about the merits of income annuities. In this chapter we will briefly review the history of annuities, or "annua" as the Romans called them, and then we will dig into the more than half a dozen types of annuities that are available.

Types of Annuities

When someone says they don't like annuities, we always ask them "Which of the 30 types of annuities or the 150 annuity companies are you talking about?" That typically makes them think about how asinine that statement might be.

It would be hard to cover the more than 30 types of annuities that are available, so we are going to cover the most common types that are available and that we discuss for utilization or exclusion with our clients.

- There are 3 main distinctions to make:
- Deferred annuities vs. Income annuities:
- Fixed annuities vs. Variable annuities.
- Hybrid fixed indexed annuities:

Deferred vs. IncomeAnnuities

Deferred annuities are annuities where the clients provides a lump sum premium and they can "invest" this premium in either a fixed interest rate, an index, or both. The client can decide to turn payments on from the annuity at a future date. They can also decide to not take payments and just let the annuity grow tax-deferred. At the end of the 2-12 year period, they can decide to take all of the remaining principal and interest and:

- Turn it into income
- Leave it with the annuity company and let it continue to compound
- 1035 exchange it into another like IRA or other retirement account vehicle (A 1035 exchange, also known as a like-kind exchange, is a legal way to swap one insurance policy, annuity, endowment or long-term care product of like kind without triggering tax on any investment

gains associated with the original contract. The IRS allows these exchanges under Section 1035 of the Internal Revenue Code.

- Start to receive just the required minimum distributions from the annuity
- Put it in their bank account (depending on the taxable nature of the annuity)

There are two types of fixed annuities: Multiyear guaranteed annuities and Fixed Indexed annuities.

Multiyear Guaranteed Annuities (MYGAs)

A MYGA (Multi-Year Guaranteed Annuity) is a type of fixed annuity contract offered by insurance companies. It guarantees a fixed interest rate for a specified number of years, typically ranging from three to ten years. During this period, the annuity holder's principal is protected, and the interest rate does not change. MYGAs are often used as a conservative investment option, providing a predictable income stream and preserving capital.

Key features of a MYGA include:

1. Guaranteed Interest Rates: The interest rate is fixed and guaranteed for the duration of the contract term. This can be from 2 – 10 years.
2. Principal Protection: The principal amount invested is protected and not subject to market fluctuations.
3. Tax-Deferred Growth: Earnings grow tax-deferred until withdrawn, potentially reducing the immediate tax liability.
4. Surrender Charges: Early withdrawals before the end of the term may incur surrender charges.
5. Renewal Options: At the end of the term, the annuity holder may have options to renew the contract, withdraw the funds, or transfer them to another annuity or investment.
6. Death Benefit: Similar to life insurance contracts, 401ks, or IRAs, if you pass away before the annuity matures, or if you let the annuity remain with the company for additional years, if you pass away, your

listed beneficiaries will get the full remaining principal plus all the interest credited.

MYGAs are often chosen by individuals seeking a low-risk investment option with predictable returns, particularly those nearing or in retirement.

Fixed Indexed Annuities

We call FIAs hybrid, guaranteed indexed products because there are over two hundred options available within them to grow your money while still protecting it. Fixed indexed annuities (FIAs) are a type of annuity that offers a combination of fixed and variable features, aiming to provide the security of principal protection with the potential for higher returns linked to the performance of a specified market index. Here's an overview of fixed indexed annuities:

Key Features:

1. Principal Protection Guarantee: The principal amount invested in an FIA is protected from market downturns. Even if the linked index performs poorly, the principal is not at risk. This sounds boring until all Hell breaks lose and everyone who isn't in FIAs is losing 20-50% of their retirement accounts.

2. Indexed Interest Captured & Credited on an Annual Basis: Returns can be based on the performance of a specific market index (e.g., S&P 500), or they can be based on a declared interest rate that is available within the annuity, or any combination of indexes and interest rates. Interest credits are added to the annuity's value based on index performance, subject to certain limitations. At the end of each 12-month period, the interest is captured, locked in, and can not be lost.

3. Cap Rate: The maximum rate of interest that can be credited in a given period, regardless of the index's performance. Cap rates have historically been a source of complaints about fixed indexed annuities. However, there are now annuities (as of the date of

publication) that have cap rates of 16%+. This cap rate level has killed off the former cap rate concerns.

4. Participation Rate: The percentage of the index gain that is credited to the annuity. For example, if the participation rate is 80% and the index gains 10%, the annuity is credited with 8%. Once again, with the evolution of the indexes, there are now indexed annuities that offer participation rates of 100 – 353% as of the date of this publication.

5. Fixed Interest Option: Fixed Interest: In addition to indexed interest, many FIAs offer a fixed interest option where a portion of the annuity can earn a guaranteed interest rate, regardless of index performance.

6. Tax-Deferred Growth: Earnings within the annuity grow tax-deferred, meaning taxes are not owed until withdrawals are made. This allows for potentially higher growth over time due to compounding.

7. Surrender Charges & Early Withdrawal Penalties: Withdrawals made before the end of a specified surrender period may incur surrender charges. These charges typically decrease over time.

8. Free Withdrawals: Some FIAs allow for penalty-free withdrawals up to a certain percentage of the account value each year. The typical ones that our team works with typically allow for up to 10% penalty-free withdrawals every year. These withdrawals are used for income, vacations, car purchases, or anything else the owner wants to use them for.

9. Income Options & Lifetime Income Riders: Many FIAs offer optional riders that provide a guaranteed lifetime income stream, which can continue even if the annuity's value is depleted.

10. Withdrawal Options: Annuitants can often choose how and when to receive income, whether through systematic withdrawals, lump-

sum payments, or converting the annuity to a lifetime income stream.

11. Death Benefit: FIAs typically provide a death benefit to beneficiaries if the annuitant passes away before the annuity is fully paid out. This can be the current account value or a guaranteed minimum amount.

Who are MYGAs, Income Annuities, and FIAs Suitable For:

- Conservative Investors: Individuals seeking principal protection with the potential for higher returns than traditional fixed annuities or CDs.
- Pre-Retirees and Retirees: Those looking for a balance of growth potential and income security in their retirement planning.
- ax-Deferred Growth: Investors looking to benefit from tax-deferred growth on their investments.

Fixed indexed annuities can be a valuable part of a diversified retirement strategy, offering a mix of security and growth potential. However, it's essential to understand the specific terms and features of the FIA being considered to ensure it aligns with individual financial goals and risk tolerance.

Income Annuities

Income annuities are purchased with a lump sum and you can have the payments start almost immediately.

Key features of Income Annuities sometimes include:

- Immediate or Deferred Income: You can have the income start next month, or you can let the money build for a few years with a plan to then turn it on later.
- Guaranteed Income for Life: The annuity company is responsible for paying you an income for the rest of your life, whether it is 40 years, 60 years, or more. People that have taken advantage of guaranteed income annuities include Shaquille O'Neal and Allen Iverson.

• Nursing Home Riders: You can add riders to the policy to double the income if you have to go into a nursing home.The interest rate is fixed and guaranteed for the duration of the contract term. Principal Protection**: The principal amount invested is protected and not subject to market fluctuations.

Shaquille O'Neal on income annuities:

"I don't pay any attention to the money. If I lose it all, it is no big deal, myself and my family are already financially secure because when I started in the NBA, every year I invested in annuities. Annuities now provide more income than myself and my family need. The money I earn now is just for fun."

Are you going to argue with Shaq and his annuity strategy? We certainly will not.

Variable Annuities:

Variable annuities are variable, which means they can make you money, and they can lose your money. These annuities allow for investment in various sub-accounts that are similar to mutual funds. The payments vary based on the performance of the investments chosen. Variable annuities can sometimes make more money than fixed indexed annuities. When you add all the fees up, variable annuities can typically end up charging fees in the 1.5 – 4.4% range with all fees included.

Deferred Income Annuities:

With deferred income annuities, you can set the payments to start at a future date. They can also be fixed or variable and often have tax-deferred growth until withdrawal.

Pros and Cons of Annuities

Pros of Annuities

1. Guaranteed Income:

- Provides a steady, predictable income stream, which can be particularly beneficial during retirement.

2. Tax Deferral:

- For deferred annuities, earnings grow tax-deferred until withdrawals begin, potentially allowing the investment to grow more rapidly than a taxable account.

3. Variety of Options:

- A wide range of annuity types caters to different financial goals and risk tolerances.

4. Death Benefit:

- Many annuities offer a death benefit, ensuring that the beneficiary receives at least the amount originally invested.

5. Principal Protection:

- Fixed and indexed annuities often provide guarantees that protect the principal from market losses.

<u>Cons of Annuities</u>

1. Fees and Expenses:

Variable annuities can have high fees, including administrative fees, mortality and expense risk charges. Fixed Indexed annuities typically do not charge any fee unless you choose to allocate part of your money to certain indexes that are available within the fixed indexed annuity. We typically do not recommend fixed indexed annuities with fees unless they are specifically for specific income requirement down the line or if the client wants a death benefit enhancement. MYGAs typically have zero fees. All annuities typically charge a surrender charges for early withdrawals over 5-10% of the current amount of the annuity per year. You can find the surrender charges in the illustrations that the licensed professional that you are working with provides.

2. Complexity:

The variety of options and features can make annuities difficult to understand and compare. This is why speaking with a knowledgeable expert on the following is crucial:

- Which annuity company?
- Which annuity?
- Which index or crediting strategy?
- Which riders should we take?
- Which fees should we pay (if any)?
- What are the guarantees in the contract?
- Is Zero my Hero (if market drops, will my maximum loss be zero)?
- How much can I withdraw each year without penalties?
- Which duration (2 – 14 years)?

3. Liquidity Issues:

- Annuities often come with restrictions on when and how you can withdraw funds. Early withdrawals can incur penalties. But many of them feature at least 10% per year withdrawals. And at least (as of the time of publication) one currently features a 20% per year withdrawal option.

4. Limited Growth Potential:

- Fixed annuities, while safe, may sometimes offer lower returns compared to other investment vehicles. This is why it is so important to understand:

- The index the money is going in
- The participation rates
- The cap rates
- The current performance of the index
- The renewal rate history of the index (i.e. how much you will get going forward each year in return)
- The annual declared interest rate options (for fixed hybrid annuities)

5. Inflation Risk:

- For immediate annuities that offer fixed payments, the payments might not keep up with inflation, reducing purchasing power over time. This is why we typically couple immediate annuities (when appropriate) with fixed hybrid solutions that can be indexed to a stock market index like the S&P 500 Index.

Protections: Creditor, Lawsuit, and Stock Market Loss Protections

Creditor Protections

Annuities can offer varying levels of protection from creditors, depending on state laws. In many states, annuities are protected to some extent from claims by creditors in the event of bankruptcy or other legal judgments. This makes them attractive for asset protection purposes.

Lawsuit Protections

Similar to creditor protections, annuities may provide some level of protection from lawsuits. State-specific laws determine the extent to which annuity assets are shielded from legal judgments. Generally, annuities can offer some degree of protection, but it's essential to understand the specific laws in your state.

Protections from Loss from the Stock Market

- Fixed Annuities: Provide complete protection from market volatility since the return is guaranteed and independent of market performance.
- Indexed Annuities: Offer partial protection from stock market losses. They provide a guaranteed minimum return and the potential for higher returns based on market index performance. However, the returns are often capped.
- Variable Annuities: Do not protect against market losses. The value of the annuity fluctuates with the performance of the underlying investments. However, riders can be purchased to offer some degree of

downside protection, such as minimum guaranteed withdrawals or income benefits.

How do annuity companies make money?

Similar to banks, some annuity companies subtract a spread (or margin) from the index gain before applying the participation rate. They also can sometimes invest the money at a higher rate of return than the interest they are required to credit the annuity.

Conclusion

Annuities can be a valuable tool for retirement planning, offering guaranteed income, tax deferral, and various other benefits. However, they come with complexities, fees, and potential downsides that need careful consideration. Understanding the types of annuities, their pros and cons, and the protections they offer against creditors, lawsuits, and market losses can help individuals make informed decisions about incorporating annuities into their financial planning strategies. It's also crucial to consider state-specific laws regarding creditor and lawsuit protections to maximize the benefits and security annuities can provide.

CHAPTER 26

ESTATE PLANNING

The Key Question:

Do you love your family? Yeah?? Prove it by being an adult and taking care of the estate planning process. Or, do you love money? Probate can cost you or your family up to 10% of the estate, so it's a good idea to nip as much of it in the bud as you possibly can.

Summary

Estate planning is a critical component of financial planning, especially for those committed to building and preserving wealth for future generations. For the Black community, estate planning not only ensures the efficient transfer of wealth but can also help to address historical disparities in terms of asset transfers, and it can empower families with financial security and a legacy. This chapter will guide you through the essentials of estate planning, helping you understand its importance and how to effectively implement estate planning for your family.

Understanding Estate Planning

Estate planning involves making arrangements for the management and disposal of your estate during your life and after death. Your estate includes everything you own including:

- Real estate
- Automobiles
- Personal property
- Investments
- Annuities
- Bank accounts
- Cryptocurrency
- Life Insurance

The primary goal of estate planning is to ensure that your wishes are honored, your loved ones are provided for, and your assets are distributed efficiently and according to your desires.

The Importance of Estate Planning (before all hell breaks lose)

1. Protecting Your Loved Ones: Estate planning ensures that your family and loved ones are taken care of financially. It can designate guardians for minor children, provide for special needs family members, and protect your spouse and kids from financial hardship.

2. Minimizing Taxes and Costs: Proper estate planning can minimize the taxes and legal fees associated with the transfer of your assets. This helps maximize the wealth passed on to your heirs. Without estate planning, up to 8-10% of your estate can go down the drain in attorney and probate fees.

3. Avoiding Probate: Probate is the legal process through which a deceased person's will is validated and their estate is distributed. It can be lengthy and costly. Effective estate planning can help avoid or streamline the probate process.

4. Ensuring Privacy: Unlike the public process of probate, a well-structured estate plan can keep your affairs private.

5. Preventing Family Disputes: This may be most important benefit of all! Clear instructions and legally binding documents can prevent disagreements and downright Civil Wars among family members about the distribution of your assets.

How can your family also avoid disputes and build multi-generational wealth at the same time? Fully fund permanent life insurance policies that will pay out upon your loved one's passing and distribute funds (potentially) tax-free to beneficiaries.

Key Components of an Estate Plan

1. Will: A will is a legal document that outlines your wishes regarding the distribution of your assets and the care of any minor children. It is the cornerstone of any estate plan.

2. Trusts: Trusts are legal entities that hold and manage assets on behalf of beneficiaries. They offer greater flexibility and control over asset distribution and can help avoid probate. Common types of trusts include:

   a. Revocable Living Trust: Allows you to retain control over the trust assets during your lifetime and specifies how they should be managed after your death.
   b. Irrevocable Trust: Cannot be changed or revoked after its creation and offers significant tax advantages.
   c. Special Needs Trust: Provides for a disabled beneficiary without affecting their eligibility for government benefits.

3. Power of Attorney: This document appoints someone to manage your financial affairs if you become incapacitated and can't make decisions for yourself.

4. Healthcare Directive: Also known as a living will or medical power of attorney, this document lays out your wishes regarding medical treatment, and it appoints someone to make healthcare decisions on your behalf.

5. Beneficiary Designations: Ensure that your retirement accounts, life insurance policies, and other accounts with beneficiary designations are updated and align with your overall estate plan.

Steps to Create an Estate Plan

1. Assess Your Assets: Make a comprehensive list of all your assets, including real estate, bank accounts, investments, insurance policies, and personal property.

2. Determine Your Goals: Define what you want to achieve with your estate plan. Consider your family's needs, your charitable intentions, and any specific bequests you want to make.

3. Consult Professionals: Work with an estate planning attorney, retirement planner, and tax professional to create a legally sound plan that is also tax-efficient.

4. Draft and Execute Documents: Create and sign all necessary legal documents, including your will, trusts, power of attorney, and healthcare directives.

5. Communicate Your Plan: Discuss your estate plan with your family and any appointed representatives to ensure everyone understands your wishes.

6. Fund your Trust: If you have created a trust for estate purposes, you will need to "move" the assets into the trust through updated deeds, beneficiaries, and more.

7. Review and Update Regularly: Life changes, such as marriage, divorce, the birth of a child, or the acquisition of significant assets can bring about the need for updates to your estate plan. Review it regularly to ensure it still meets your goals.

Overcoming Common Barriers to Estate Planning

The biggest barrier regarding estate planning and the Black community is that many people want to put their heads in the sand. One client that we're working with has an 84-year old Mother who is suffering from cancer but who still refuses to get any estate planning done. She simply wants to ignore the realities of needing to put some planning in place.

Here are some other barriers to estate planning:

1. Lack of Awareness: Many people underestimate the importance of estate planning or believe it's only for the wealthy.

2. Procrastination: Estate planning can be complex and emotionally challenging, leading to delays. Start small, setting aside time to tackle each component of your plan step-by-step.

3. Cost Concerns: While hiring professionals can be expensive, the costs of not planning—such as legal fees, taxes, and family disputes—can be much higher. Seek out community organizations that offer affordable estate planning services.

The Summary for Estate Planning

For the Black community, estate planning is not just about wealth transfer; it's about empowerment and creating a legacy of financial stability.

Here are some specific strategies to consider:

1. Educate and Involve the Next Generation: Teach your children and grandchildren about financial literacy and the importance of estate planning. Involve them in the planning process to ensure they understand and can carry forward your legacy.

2. Support Black-Owned Businesses and Charities: Consider incorporating charitable giving into your estate plan. Establishing a charitable trust or foundation can support causes important to you and the community AND still be exceptionally tax-efficient for you as you build and preserve wealth.

3. Leverage Life Insurance: Life insurance can be a powerful tool for wealth transfer, providing a tax-free death benefit to your heirs. It can also fund trusts and provide liquidity to pay estate taxes or other expenses.

Conclusion

Estate planning is a vital step in building and preserving wealth within the Black community. By taking the time to create a comprehensive estate plan, you protect your loved ones, minimize taxes and costs, and ensure your legacy endures for generations. Start today by assessing your assets, defining your goals, and seeking professional guidance. Your future, and the future of your family, depends on it.

CHAPTER 27

LIFE INSURANCE

The Reality

The reality of life insurance in America: Most Americans (of all hues) are drastically underinsured. And many American families are one accident or death away from facing financial ruin because a spouse or head of household didn't properly insure themselves.

Listen to me very clearly: If you have dependents, you still have a mortgage, or you have a spouse that is counting on your income in retirement, you need to have at least $500,000 in life insurance. We would prefer if you had $1 million. We can not stress this enough.

If you have children under the age of 18, if you still have a mortgage, if you're still trying to save for your kids' education, or if your spouse and household are counting on your income to make ends meet for the next 50 years, and you have less than $500,000, your family is in grave danger of financial ruin (i.e. running out of money and becoming destitute). Over the last 15 years, we have seen way too many cases and examples where people were drastically underinsured and their families have:

- Lost their homes
- Seen their kids' college wishes go up in smoke
- Become financially distressed

The Basics

Life insurance can play a significant role in estate planning. It ensures that your heirs receive a tax-free inheritance, helping to preserve your wealth for future generations.

How much Life Insurance do you Need to Secure your Family? How much do you need to secure your family, your kids, or other loved ones for 25+ years?

The quick analysis says 5x – 10x your annual salary or annual worth (in the case of a parent that is staying home to watch the kids, do the dishes, cook meals, take the kids to soccer practice, and more).

Generally speaking, for anyone making at least $50,000 per year, they should apply for $1,000,000.

That might sound crazy until:

- You think about inflation
- You take a 5% rate of return on $1,000,000, and that's only $50,000 per year that your family can safely use from the policy to fund their annual lifestyle.

So, if you are currently making $200,000, you potentially need $4,000,000 in life insurance.

Peace of Mind

Knowing that you and your loved ones are financially protected provides peace of mind. This emotional security allows you to focus on your financial goals without constantly worrying about unexpected setbacks.

Life Insurance Tips and Best Practices

1. Regularly Review Your Coverage: As your life circumstances change, your insurance needs may change as well. Periodically review your policies to ensure they still align with your goals and circumstances.

2. Seek Professional Advice: Consult with insurance professionals or financial advisors to determine the right coverage for your specific situation. They can help you find the best policies at the most affordable rates.

3. Consider Bundling: Some insurance providers offer discounts when you bundle multiple types of insurance, such as auto and homeowners insurance. Bundling can help you save money.

4. Maintain a Healthy Lifestyle: A healthy lifestyle can often lead to lower insurance premiums, especially for health and life insurance. Quitting smoking, maintaining a healthy weight, and regular exercise can positively impact your rates.

Conclusion

Insurance is an essential pillar of wealth building and preservation. By protecting your assets and securing your family's financial future, you can continue on the path to building Black wealth with confidence. Don't view insurance as an expense but as an investment in your financial security and legacy. In the next chapter, we will explore another vital aspect of wealth preservation—estate planning.

CHAPTER 28

JUVENILE LIFE INSURANCE

Introduction

Building wealth within the Black community requires innovative and strategic approaches, particularly when it comes to securing the financial future of our children. One often-overlooked strategy is the use of life insurance as a savings vehicle and a means of financial support for college education. This chapter will explore the benefits, methods, and best practices for utilizing life insurance policies to enhance the financial stability and opportunities for our children.

Understanding Life Insurance as a Savings Tool

Life insurance policies, particularly whole life and universal life insurance, can serve as more than just a safety net in the event of untimely death. These policies accumulate cash value over time, which can be accessed and used for various purposes, including funding your child's education.

1. Types of Life Insurance:

- **Whole Life Insurance**: Provides coverage for the insured's entire life, with a guaranteed death benefit and a cash value component that grows at a guaranteed rate.
- **Universal Life Insurance**: Offers more flexibility, with adjustable premiums and death benefits, and a cash value component that can grow based on market interest rates.

For children's policies, our clear preference until otherwise proven or noted is whole life insurance.

More specifically, 5-year, 8-year, or 10-year paid up policy options.

Benefits of Using Life Insurance for Savings and College Funding

1. Guaranteed Growth: Whole life insurance policies guarantee a minimum rate of return on the cash value, providing a safe and predictable growth of savings.

2. Tax Advantages: The cash value growth in a life insurance policy is tax-deferred. Additionally, policy loans taken against the cash value are generally tax-free, offering a cost-effective way to access funds.

3. Financial Security: Beyond savings, life insurance provides a death benefit that can ensure your child's financial security in case of unexpected events.

Steps to Implementing Life Insurance for Your Child's Future

1. Assessing Your Needs and Goals: Determine how much you can afford to contribute to a policy and what your long-term financial goals are for your child. Consider factors such as projected college costs and potential financial emergencies.
2. Choosing the Right Policy: Work with a financial advisor or insurance agent to select a policy that aligns with your goals. Whole life policies are often preferred for their stability and guaranteed growth.
3. Regular Contributions: Treat your life insurance premium payments as a crucial part of your financial plan. Consistent contributions ensure the cash value grows steadily.
4. Monitoring and Adjusting: Periodically review the policy's performance and your financial situation. Adjust premiums or policy features as needed to stay on track with your goals.

Utilizing the Cash Value for College and Other Needs

You have to know how to practice the withdrawals from these policies. With that said, here are the options:

1. Policy Loans: Most life insurance policies allow you to borrow against the cash value. This can be a valuable resource for paying college tuition, buying books, or covering living expenses. Loans do not need to be repaid immediately, but interest will accrue, and the outstanding loan amount will be deducted from the death benefit if not repaid.

2. Withdrawals: Some policies permit direct withdrawals from the cash value. While withdrawals can reduce the policy's death benefit, they can be a useful tool for funding education or other major expenses.

3.*Strategic Timing: Plan withdrawals or loans to minimize the impact on the policy's growth. Ideally, use these funds only when necessary to preserve the maximum benefit for the future.

Conclusion

Leveraging life insurance as a savings vehicle and financial support tool for college can play a critical role in building Black wealth and securing the financial future of our children. By understanding the types of life insurance, the benefits, and the practical steps for implementation, families can make informed decisions that align with their long-term financial goals. This strategy not only provides immediate financial benefits but also contributes to the generational wealth and stability of the Black community.

Action Steps

1. Consult with an independent insurance broker or financial advisor: Seek professional guidance to choose the best policy for your family.

2. Start Early: The earlier you start, the more time your policy has to grow and provide substantial benefits for your child's future.

By incorporating life insurance into your financial strategy, you can create a robust plan for building wealth and supporting your children's education, contributing to a brighter and more secure future for the next generation.

CHAPTER 29

ALTERNATIVE INVESTMENTS & CRYPTO

For individuals with under $2 million in investable assets, diversification into alternative investments can be a prudent strategy to enhance returns, reduce risk, and provide income stability long term.

What Are Alternative Investments?

Alternative investments are assets that fall outside the traditional categories of stocks, bonds, and cash. They are considered alternative because they offer different risk-return profiles and often have low correlations with the broader financial markets.

Section 1: Why Consider Alternative Investments?

Diversification and Risk Management

Alternative investments can help diversify your portfolio, spreading risk across different asset classes. Since they often don't move in tandem with traditional investments, they can act as a hedge against market volatility.

Potential for Higher Returns

Some alternative investments have shown the potential for significant returns. Cryptocurrency, for example, has seen substantial growth in recent years. However, it's essential to note that higher returns come with higher risk.

Non-Correlation with Traditional Markets

Like annuities, many alternative investments, such as art and wine, are not directly tied to stock and bond markets and provide asymmetric returns to the financial markets. This non-correlation can provide stability during market downturns.

Section 2: Exploring Different Types of Alternative Investments

Here are several alternative investment options that may be suitable:

1. **Real Estate**
    - Rental Properties: Investing in residential or commercial rental properties can provide a steady income stream and potential for property value appreciation.
    - Real Estate Investment Trusts (REITs): REITs offer a way to invest in real estate without the need to manage properties directly. They can provide dividend income and portfolio diversification.
    - Crowdfunding Platforms: Real estate crowdfunding allows investors to pool funds with others to invest in larger real estate projects, which can offer higher returns with lower initial capital requirements.

2. **Peer-to-Peer Lending**
    - - P2P Lending Platforms: Platforms like LendingClub or Prosper (as examples only) can enable individuals to lend money to others in exchange for interest payments. This can offer higher yields than traditional savings accounts or bonds, though it comes with higher risk including the risk of losing all of your principal.

3. **Private Equity and Venture Capital**
    - Equity Crowdfunding: Equity crowdfunding platforms like SeedInvest or Fundrise allow smaller investors to buy shares in private companies or startups, providing exposure to potential high-growth opportunities.
    - Angel Investing: Investing in early-stage startups can be lucrative, but it requires significant due diligence and carries high risk including the loss of your entire principal.

4. **Commodities**

• Precious Metals: Investing in gold, silver, or other precious metals can serve as a hedge against inflation and economic instability.

• Commodity ETFs: These funds track the performance of various commodities, offering a way to gain exposure without directly buying physical commodities.

5. **Hedge Funds and Mutual Funds**

• Hedge Fund-like Mutual Funds: Some mutual funds employ strategies similar to hedge funds, such as long/short equity, market neutral, or global macro strategies. These can offer diversification benefits.

• Fund of Funds: Investing in a fund that itself invests in multiple hedge funds can provide exposure to diverse strategies with lower minimum investment requirements than direct hedge fund investments.

6. **Cryptocurrencies**

• Bitcoin and Altcoins: Investing in cryptocurrencies like Bitcoin and Ethereum can offer high returns, though they are highly volatile and speculative… Treat them like hand grenades.

• Bitcoin and Ethereum ETFs (exchanged traded funds) – As of 2024 there are now over a dozen Bitcoin and Ethereum ETFs that are available for trade on the NASDAQ and NYSE among other exchanges. If you Google "List of cryptocurrency ETFs", dozens of crypto ETFs will come up.

• Crypto Funds: Funds that invest in a basket of cryptocurrencies or blockchain-related companies can offer diversified exposure to the crypto market. Once again, as with all other investment strategies, this route can be lucrative or highly risky.

7. **Collectibles and Tangibles**

• Art, Antiques, and Collectibles: Investing in art, antiques, wine, or other collectibles can be a store of value and offer substantial appreciation potential.

- Wine: Specific wines and distributions from specific wineries can yield substantial returns on investment over time.
- Rare Coins and Stamps: These can be valuable over time, though they require expertise to invest effectively.

Section 3: Risks and Considerations

It's important to acknowledge that alternative investments come with unique risks and considerations:

Illiquidity: Some alternative investments may not be easily convertible to cash, making them less suitable for short-term needs.

Lack of Regulation: Many alternative investments are less regulated than traditional assets, which can expose investors to fraud and market manipulation.

Expertise Required: Successfully investing in alternatives often requires specialized knowledge or access to professionals with expertise in the specific asset class.

Section 4: Incorporating Alternatives into Your Portfolio

Determine Your Risk Tolerance: Before adding alternative investments, assess your risk tolerance and overall financial goals. Consider working with a financial advisor to find the right balance.

Start Small: If you're new to alternative investments, consider starting with a small allocation to gain experience and confidence.

Stay Informed: Keep abreast of market trends and developments in your chosen alternative asset class. Continuous learning is key to success.

Resources

Podcasts for alternative investment info including info on peer-to-peer lending, real estate, and cryptocurrency – The Cash Flow Ninja;

for Real Estate and real estate lending information – Bigger Pockets

Conclusion

Alternative investments can be a valuable addition to your wealth-building strategy, providing diversification and the potential for higher returns. However, they also come with unique risks and complexities. As you explore these opportunities, it's essential to approach them with caution, seek expert advice when needed, and ensure they align with your overall financial goals.

CHAPTER 30

TAX REDUCTION

The Quick Summary for Retirement Accounts & Taxation:

Please consult with a tax advisor, and please remember you are an adult so you can make your own decisions. Here are some options to consider:

1. Get the match from your company.
2. With all remaining discretionary funds, max out your individual Roth IRA or the Roth inside a TSP (Thrift Savings Plan) if you are a federal employee or have access to a Roth inside your organization
3. Once the Roth IRA is maxed out, consider setting 20-25% of your discretionary savings aside in a permanent cash value life insurance structures where you can withdraw the cash value in a tax-free manner if done correctly.
4. If you have qualified accounts that are pre-tax (401ks, TSPs, IRAs, 403bs or 457s), and if you are in the 24% or lower tax brackets (as of 2024), consider Roth conversions that keep your tax rate at 24% or under.

"The number one expense for most people is taxes."
– Robert Kiyosaki, Rich Dad Poor Dad author

Taxes play one of the most important roles in the wealth building & financial planning landscape, especially for those nearing retirement or looking to build wealth. Understanding the intricacies of taxes and implementing effective tax reduction strategies can significantly impact your financial well-being. This chapter aims to provide comprehensive insights into taxes and practical strategies to minimize tax liabilities while maximizing wealth.

The Basics of Taxes and Their Impact on Wealth

Taxes are compulsory financial charges imposed by governments on income, businesses, property, and transactions. They are the primary source of revenue for public services and infrastructure, which is what they are supposed to be used for. For individuals, taxes are typically levied on earned income, investment income, and capital gains. Understanding the different types of taxes and how they affect your finances is crucial for effective wealth building.

If you explain taxes to a child, they will often say that taxes sound a lot like "theft." We are not here to argue with intelligent children, so their point is well taken. Consider these statistics from TaxFoundation.org:

- The top 1 percent of taxpayers paid a 25.9 percent average rate, nearly eight times higher than the 3.3 percent average rate paid by the bottom half of taxpayers.
- The top 1 percent's income share rose from 22.2 percent in 2020 to 26.3 percent in 2021 and its share of federal income taxes paid rose from 42.3 percent to 45.8 percent.
- The top 50 percent of all taxpayers paid 97.7 percent of all federal individual income taxes
- The bottom 50 percent paid the remaining 2.3 percent.

Bottom line: If you make more money, you may pay more taxes not just on a pure scale but from a percentage scale as well.

Is that fair? We'll let you ponder that, but we certainly think it makes sense to pay utilize tax-efficient strategies when building wealth and trying to make sure you **don't run out of money in retirement**.

You can also question whether it's fair for higher income earners to get taxed on up to 85% of their Social Security payments, or for them to pay up to **350% more for Medicare Part B & D coverage**.

So, are taxes boring? Yes.

Can an efficient, intelligent strategy around taxation make your life spicier? Absolutely yes.

<u>What type of taxes exist</u>?

1. Income Taxes: These are taxes on earnings from employment, business operations, and other sources of income. They can be progressive (increasing with higher income levels) or flat (a single rate for all income levels). Income taxes can be at the federal level, state level, or even the municipal level.
    a. States with no income tax currently include:
        i. Alaska
        ii. Florida
        iii. Nevada
        iv. New Hampshire (doesn't tax earned wages, but does tax investment earnings)
        v. South Dakota
        vi. Tennessee
        vii. Texas
        viii. Washington
        ix. Wyoming

However, if a state doesn't have an income tax, they may try to "make up for it" with higher sales taxes or property taxes for example.

2. Capital Gains Taxes: These are taxes on the profit from the sale of assets such as stocks, bonds, or real estate. Long-term capital gains (on assets held for more than a year) often have lower tax rates than short-term capital gains.

3. Estate and Inheritance Taxes: These taxes are levied on the transfer of wealth from deceased individuals to their heirs. They can significantly reduce the amount of wealth passed on to future generations.

4. Property Taxes: Property taxes are local taxes imposed on real estate by local governments, such as counties, cities, and school districts. These taxes are a significant source of revenue for local governments, funding essential public services like schools, roads, police, and fire departments.

5. Sales Taxes: These are taxes that are added on to almost everything you purchase, be it in a supermarket, a car dealership, or a cookie shop.

6. Penny Taxes for infrastructure: In addition to charging property taxes to fund road and other projects, some counties may charge an additional one or two cents per bill or per gallon to fund transportation projects.

Retirement & Tax-Advantaged Accounts

When it comes to building wealth, it's really important to understand the difference between pre-tax deductions from your paycheck and tax deferral vs. post-tax investments that will be tax-free in terms of the growth and taxation of the account going forward after a 5-year period.

Utilizing tax-advantaged accounts is a cornerstone strategy for minimizing taxes and maximizing wealth growth. These accounts offer tax benefits that can help you save more efficiently for retirement and other financial goals.

1. Individual Retirement Accounts (IRAs):

- Traditional IRAs: Contributions may be tax-deductible, and earnings grow tax-deferred. Taxes are paid upon withdrawal during retirement.
- Roth IRAs: Contributions are made with after-tax dollars, but earnings grow tax-free, and qualified withdrawals are tax-free. With Roth IRAs, we say that you are paying tax on the seed, but not on the full harvest.

2. 401(k), TSP, 403(b), 457 Plans: Employer-sponsored retirement plans that allow employees to contribute pre-tax income. Employers may

offer matching contributions, providing an additional boost to retirement savings. Earnings grow tax-deferred, with taxes paid upon withdrawal.

3. Health Savings Accounts (HSAs): Available to individuals with high-deductible health plans, HSAs offer triple tax advantages: contributions are tax-deductible, earnings grow tax-free, and withdrawals for qualified medical expenses are tax-free.

Strategic Tax Planning for Retirement

Effective tax planning is essential for retirees to ensure that their savings last throughout retirement while minimizing tax liabilities.

Here are some key strategies:

1. Roth Conversions: Converting traditional IRA funds to a Roth IRA can be advantageous, especially in years when your taxable income is lower. While the conversion itself is a taxable event, future earnings and withdrawals from the Roth IRA are tax-free.

2024 tax information

Income taxes[1]

Single

Taxable income	Tax rate
$0-$11,600	**10%** of taxable income
$11,601-$47,150	$1,160 plus **12%** of the excess over $11,600
$47,151-$100,525	$5,426 plus **22%** of the excess over $47,150
$100,526-$191,950	$17,168.50 plus **24%** of the excess over $100,525
$191,951-$243,725	$39,110.50 plus **32%** of the excess over $191,950
$243,726-$609,350	$55,678.50 plus **35%** of the excess over $243,725
$609,351+	$183,647.25 plus **37%** of the excess over $609,350

Married filing jointly or qualifying widow(er)

Taxable income	Tax rate
$0-$23,200	**10%** of taxable income
$23,201-$94,300	$2,320 plus **12%** of the excess over $23,200
$94,301-$201,050	$10,852 plus **22%** of the excess over $94,300
$201,051-$383,900	$34,337 plus **24%** of the excess over $201,050
$383,901-$487,450	$78,221 plus **32%** of the excess over $383,900
$487,451-$731,200	$111,357 plus **35%** of the excess over $487,450
$731,201+	$196,669.50 plus **37%** of the excess over $731,200

2. Tax-Efficient Withdrawal Strategies: Do you have an exit plan?? Developing a strategy for withdrawing funds from various accounts can help manage tax liabilities. For instance, withdrawing from taxable accounts first can allow tax-advantaged accounts to continue growing. Also, for example, if you are working and getting taxed in the 32% bracket, but want to retire and start living off of money in your retirement accounts, you may want to wait until January 1 rolls around to pull the money out (ostensibly in a lower tax rate environment) so that you can pay less taxes on your withdrawals.

3. Qualified Charitable Distributions (QCDs): Retirees aged 70½ or older can make tax-free charitable donations directly from their IRAs. QCDs can satisfy required minimum distributions (RMDs) without increasing taxable income.

4. Charitable deductions: If you are going to contribute amounts that are over and above the standard deduction for a single person or a couple, then you can consider itemizing the deduction.

5. Gifting: If you have more money than you need and would rather give money to your family than to Uncle Sam and the IRS, then the annual gift tax exclusion is a set dollar amount that you may give someone without needing to report it to the IRS. The threshold is typically adjusted to account for inflation each year. The IRS announced that the annual gift tax exclusion will be $18,000 in 2024, up from $17,000 in 2023.

Besides these options for tax efficiency, there are more options for higher income earners or people with higher levels of assets.

<u>Charitable Remainder Trusts</u>

A Charitable Remainder Trust (CRT) is a type of irrevocable trust that provides financial benefits to both the trust's beneficiaries and a designated charity. It allows the donor to receive income from the trust for a specified period, after which the remaining assets are transferred to the chosen charity. This arrangement offers significant tax benefits while supporting philanthropic goals.

Donor Advised Funds and Retirement Tax Planning Opportunities

A Donor Advised Fund (DAF) is a charitable giving vehicle administered by a public charity, which manages donations on behalf of individuals, families, or organizations. Donors contribute to the DAF and receive an immediate tax deduction. The funds can then be invested and grow tax-free until the donor recommends grants to qualified charitable organizations.

Key Features:

1. Immediate Tax Deduction: Donors receive a tax deduction in the year they contribute to the DAF, even if the funds are distributed to charities in future years.
2. Tax-Free Growth: Investments within the DAF grow tax-free, potentially increasing the amount available for charitable giving.
3. Flexibility in Giving: Donors can recommend grants to various charities over time, providing flexibility and strategic planning in their philanthropy.

Tax Benefits:

1. Reduction of Taxable Income: Contributions to a DAF reduce taxable income in the year of the donation, which can be particularly beneficial in high-income years.
2. Capital Gains Tax Avoidance: Donating appreciated securities directly to a DAF allows donors to avoid paying capital gains taxes on the appreciation, while still receiving a charitable deduction for the full market value of the securities.

Retirement Tax Planning Opportunities

Tax planning is a critical component of retirement planning, aiming to minimize tax liabilities and maximize the longevity of retirement savings. Here are some key strategies:

1. **Roth Conversions**:

• Roth IRA: Converting a Traditional IRA to a Roth IRA involves paying taxes on the converted amount now, rather than during retirement. This can be beneficial if you expect to be in a higher tax bracket in the future or if you want to reduce required minimum distributions (RMDs) in retirement.

• Tax Diversification: Having both Traditional and Roth accounts can provide flexibility in managing taxable income in retirement.

2. **Tax-Efficient Withdrawal Strategies**:

• Order of Withdrawals: Strategic withdrawals from taxable accounts, Traditional IRAs, and Roth IRAs can minimize taxes. Typically, it's advantageous to withdraw from taxable accounts first, then tax-deferred accounts, and lastly from Roth accounts.

• Managing RMDs: Planning ahead to manage RMDs from Traditional IRAs and 401(k)s can help avoid large taxable distributions.

3. **Qualified Charitable Distributions** (QCDs):

• Direct Transfers: For individuals aged 70½ or older, QCDs allow direct transfers from an IRA to a qualified charity, which can satisfy RMDs without increasing taxable income.

• Annual Limit: Up to $100,000 per year can be transferred tax-free via QCDs.

4. **Health Savings Accounts** (HSAs):

• Triple Tax Advantage: HSAs offer a triple tax benefit: contributions are tax-deductible, growth is tax-free, and withdrawals for qualified medical expenses are tax-free.

• Retirement Medical Expenses: HSAs can be a powerful tool to save for medical expenses in retirement, reducing the overall tax burden.

5. **Charitable Giving**:

• Bunching Donations: Donors can "bunch" multiple years' worth of charitable contributions into one year to exceed the standard deduction threshold, allowing them to itemize deductions and receive a greater tax benefit.

• Donor Advised Funds: As mentioned, DAFs can be used to facilitate strategic charitable giving and maximize tax benefits.

By incorporating these strategies, individuals can better manage their tax liabilities and enhance their financial security in retirement. Always consult with a financial advisor or tax professional to tailor these strategies to your specific circumstances.

<u>Types of CRTs</u> (Charitable Remainder Trusts)

1. Charitable Remainder Annuity Trust (CRAT): Provides a fixed annual income to the beneficiaries, which does not change regardless of the trust's performance. The payout must be at least 5% of the initial value of the trust's assets.

2. Charitable Remainder Unitrust (CRUT): Provides a variable annual income to the beneficiaries, which is a fixed percentage (at least 5%) of the trust's assets as valued annually. This means the income can fluctuate based on the trust's performance.

<u>Benefits of CRTs</u>

1. Income Stream: The donor or other beneficiaries receive an income stream for life or for a specified number of years.

2. Tax Deduction: The donor receives an immediate charitable income tax deduction based on the present value of the remainder interest that will eventually go to the charity.

3. Capital Gains Tax Avoidance: Donating appreciated assets to a CRT allows the donor to avoid immediate capital gains taxes that would have been incurred if the assets were sold.

4. Estate Tax Reduction: Assets transferred to a CRT are removed from the donor's estate, potentially reducing estate taxes.

5. Philanthropic Impact: The remainder of the trust's assets benefits the chosen charity, supporting its mission and goals.

How CRTs Work

1. Establishing the Trust: The donor creates the CRT and transfers assets into the trust. These assets can include cash, stocks, real estate, or other valuable property.

2. Receiving Income: The trust provides income to the donor or other designated beneficiaries. For CRATs, this income is a fixed amount; for CRUTs, it is a percentage of the trust's value recalculated annually.

3. Trust Administration: The trust is managed by a trustee, who invests the assets and ensures the income is paid to the beneficiaries.

4. Charitable Distribution: At the end of the trust term (which can be for the life of the beneficiaries or a specified number of years), the remaining assets are distributed to the designated charity.

Example

Suppose a donor funds a CRUT with $1 million worth of appreciated stock. The trust agreement specifies that the donor will receive 5% of the trust's value annually. If the trust's assets grow, the donor's income increases, but if the assets decrease, the donor's income decreases. The donor receives an immediate income tax deduction for the present value of the remainder interest that will eventually go to the charity. After the donor's lifetime (or a specified term), the remaining assets go to the charity. However, the charity can be the donor's family foundation.

Considerations for CRTs

1. Irrevocability: Once established, a CRT cannot be modified or revoked.

2. Complexity: Setting up and managing a CRT can be complex and may require professional assistance.

3. Compliance: The trust must comply with IRS regulations to maintain its tax benefits.

*Sources: IRS on Charitable Remainder Trust, Fidelity on Charitable Trusts, Investopedia on Charitable Remainder Trusts

By establishing a CRT, donors can achieve a balance between receiving income, reducing taxes, and supporting charitable causes, making it a valuable tool in both financial and philanthropic planning.

Reducing Taxes on Investments

Investment income and capital gains can significantly impact your tax bill. Here are some strategies to minimize taxes on your investments:

1. Tax-Loss Harvesting: Selling investments at a loss to offset gains from other investments can reduce your overall tax liability. This strategy can be particularly effective in years when the market experiences volatility.

2. Holding Investments Long-Term: Long-term capital gains are generally taxed at lower rates than short-term gains. Holding investments for at least a year can reduce your tax burden.

3. Utilizing Tax-Advantaged Accounts for Investments: Holding investments in tax-advantaged accounts such as IRAs, 401(k)s, or HSAs can defer or eliminate taxes on earnings and capital gains.

Estate Planning and Wealth Transfer

Transferring wealth to future generations can be complicated by estate and inheritance taxes. Implementing effective estate planning strategies can help minimize these taxes and ensure a smooth transfer of assets.

1. Trusts: Establishing trusts can provide control over the distribution of assets and reduce estate taxes. For example, a revocable living trust can help avoid probate, while an irrevocable trust can remove assets from your taxable estate.

2. Gifting Strategies: Annual gifting allows you to transfer a certain amount of money or assets tax-free to individuals each year. This can reduce the size of your taxable estate over time.

3. Life Insurance: Using life insurance can provide a tax-free death benefit to beneficiaries, helping to cover estate taxes or replace lost income. And the best part is you can spend all of your current income and retirement savings as long as you have guaranteed income and long-

term care coverage. The life insurance can deliver everything you desire tax-free to your beneficiaries (the people you love) after you pass.

Conclusion

Building and preserving wealth requires a comprehensive understanding of taxes and strategic planning to minimize tax liabilities. By leveraging tax-advantaged accounts, implementing effective tax reduction strategies, and planning for the transfer of wealth, individuals can enhance their financial security and ensure a lasting legacy for future generations. Remember, it's always advisable to consult with a financial advisor or tax professional to tailor these strategies to your unique situation and goals.

CHAPTER 31

TAX REDUCTION IN RETIREMENT

Why the need for the IRA Rescue Plan?
In three words, TAXES, DEMOGRAPHICS, and CONTROL.

Taxes

On the tax front, at the time of publication of this critically important book, the United States federal debt stands at $36 trillion, which amounts to $107,000 in debt per citizen, but $271,000 in debt per federal taxpayer.

According to USdebtclock.org, by the year 2028 the U.S. national debt may stand at nearly $47 trillion, or nearly $334,000 per taxpayer.

With the 2017 Trump tax cuts set to potentially expire at the end of 2025, and with the United States federal tax rates at lows compared to World War II and other times when the federal government needed to drastically raise revenue, our country is likely at its very lowest federal tax point that we will see in the next 20 years.

With nearly $39 Trillion currently squirreled away in largely liquid & qualified (pre-tax) retirement accounts like 401ks, 457bs, 403bs, TSPs, and IRAs, where do you think the federal government will seek to get a large portion of revenue from to cover the debt and the interest on this debt?

In addition, many states in this country are facing structural, long-term deficits in their state budgets, and they will also be eyeing this nearly $39 Trillion worth of qualified retirement account assets to fill the budget holes. And based on the city you live in, even your city or municipality may come knocking on the door for a piece of your hard-earned 401k, TSP, or IRA since many of them are facing the same fiscal challenges that the states are facing.

Demographics

Many of you have heard these statistics, but now they are a reality. At the time of publication, every day, nearly 10,000 people are turning 65 years old in the United States. 2024 is actually the peak retirement year. While we applaud all of you that are retiring for all the hard work that you have put in, and while we are excited that many of you are finally able to hopefully enjoy your retirement, we also realize the following:

- Social Security used to be based on a 40:1 worker to retiree ratio; now it is closer to 3:1, and it was already strained
- This peak retirement phase will continue on for another 5-7 years at least
- Medicare is already strained, and the price of Medicare Part B may continue to go up due to this strain and due to inflation (was $15.50 in 1985, and is $174.70 in 2024)
- In addition to the U.S. official federal debt, based on the projection of all the people turning 65 and taking Social Security, the unfunded liabilities stand at:
    - $27 Trillion for Social Security
    - $41 Trillion for Medicare

How is the government going to pay for these programs? They will either:

- Cut benefits
- Raise the age requirements
- Provide means testing for the benefits
- Or raise taxes in other areas to fund this

There are literally no other options, unless you expect for the new Medicare and Social Security beneficiaries to vote against themselves and wind these programs down.

Control

Do you want to be in control, or do you want your tax situation to be outside of your control?

Perhaps the most compelling reason to implement the IRA Rescue Plan is so that you will have full control over your retirement savings.

And to get your retirement account silent partners (the U.S. federal government, your state government, and your local government) out of your business.

For every $1,000,000 in a qualified (pre-tax contribution) retirement account, you (the person that toiled away for 20-50 years for these assets) are typically only an 85% owner of the account, at best. Your "silent partners" in the deal typically own between 15 – 35% of the account.

You are typically the last stakeholder to get access to your funds, with the U.S. federal government, your state government, and even your municipal government stepping in line before you to take their 15-35% share of taxes before you get access to your money.

At the RMD (required minimum distribution) age, you are forced to pull money out of your account for the rest of your life.

And upon death, the "silent partners" truly back the Brinks truck up since your heirs have to officially draw down or liquidate and distribute the funds within a 10-year period, thanks to the SECURE Act. This 10-year rule can bring tax bills of 30%+, depending on who is inheriting the IRA and their tax status.

<u>The Crystal Ball</u>

As of the time of this writing, do you have any idea what the federal tax will be in the year 2028, 2029, or 2030?

Contrast that complete lack of knowledge with where we know U.S. federal debt will likely be in the year 2028, 2029, and 2030. The year 2030 is likely when the rubber will fully meet the road and the U.S. government, just to service the debt payments, will likely be forced to:

1. Raise taxes drastically
2. Cut spending drastically

If you've spent time in Washington, D.C. and the surrounding areas like I have in the last 3 years as a volunteer speaker to federal employees and federal contractors for the Foundation for Financial Education, you know that there is virtually ZERO chance that the federal government is going to drastically reduce spending.

The Washington, D.C. area is arguably the nation's richest metro area, and it has more cranes and construction going on than virtually any other part of the country. Why do you think this is?

So if the U.S. federal government is going to turn to taxing its citizens to fix the debt issue, and if the biggest bucket of $$ they can tax will be sitting in your retirement account, if you don't take control now to reposition this money to an acceptable level then it will be your fault that you didn't seize control when you had a chance.

Our team at Ready2Retire can not only help you reduce the tax liability of your retirement accounts. We can help you to potentially eliminate it (i.e. take it down to 0%) while also helping you to build a legacy, enjoy your retirement income, and have full control during your well-deserved retirement years.

Taking Action

The bottom line is that some, including many of our clients, are going to use the IRA Rescue Plan to legally take control of their retirement savings, tax situation, and the amount of their Social Security that is taxed.

Many others are going to stick their heads in the sand and hope for the best, or simply wait on the tracks until the freight train runs them completely over with tax rates that may potentially go up for decades.

Right now, you have the power, and we have the solutions. You can choose to take action and take control, or you can deal with the consequences (soon).

The decision is yours!

THE QUICK SUMMARY: THE IRA RESCUE PLAN

The IRA Rescue Plan....To The Rescue!!

The IRA Rescue plan is designed to methodically solve this problem over time with whatever portion of qualified assets that you decide you want to remove from the clutches of the Federal, state, and local tax regimes.

Yes, you will still pay federal income taxes on the distributions or conversions of these qualified assets, unless you have a very creative, law-abiding accountant or are utilizing losses from other assets (real estate for example) to offset the gains.

But you (and your family if you so choose) still win big long-term because of what the plan brings to the table.

The IRA Rescue plan repositions tax-qualified assets over to the non-taxable bucket. The plan insures that, if accessed properly, these assets will never be taxed again, and can be utilized for a number of purposed at your discretion.

And besides that, have you seen the website www.USdebtclock.org? It helps you see the roughly $1 trillion in US Debt that is added roughly every 100 days as of the date of this writing.

Even if you aren't concerned with the overall amount of US Federal, state, and local government debt as it relates to the general economy, you should be concerned about this debt (and the "debt per taxpayer" number) as it relates to your PERSONAL FUTURE ECONOMY and the amount of taxes you and your family may have to pay going forward.

CHAPTER 32

FEES

Taxes and Fees are the true enemies of wealth creation and preservation, in addition to inflation (the stealth tax) and WMDs (weapons of mass distraction).

In the quest to build and preserve Black wealth, one often underestimated aspect is the impact of fees and taxes. Over time, these seemingly small charges can erode your hard-earned money significantly. In this chapter, we will explore strategies to reduce fees and taxes across various aspects of your financial life.

Reducing Taxes in Your Personal Budget

Taxes are so important, and such a big expense (arguably the largest expense) that we are going to cover them again.

By adopting tax-efficient spending habits, you can minimize your tax liability:

- Tax-Advantaged Accounts: Contribute to retirement accounts, such as 401(k)s and IRAs, which offer tax advantages.
- Tax-free Accounts: If you are currently in lower tax brackets and have disposable savings, you should consider Roth IRAs and Roth accounts as an options to pay the tax now but forever be tax-free with those accounts later.
- Health Savings Accounts (HSAs): Use HSAs to pay for qualified medical expenses with pre-tax dollars.
- Tax Credits: Explore tax credits like the Earned Income Tax Credit (EITC) and Child Tax Credit.
- Roth Conversions prior to taking RMDs (required minimum distributions): Have a financial advisor or retirement income expert run Roth conversion charts for you to determine if this is a good idea given your projected income and current and future tax rates.

Smart Budgeting to Minimize Tax Waste

Effective budgeting is key to managing expenses and minimizing taxes:

- Track Expenses: Monitor your spending to identify areas where you can cut costs.
- Tax Deductions: Keep records of deductible expenses, such as home office expenses for self-employed individuals.

Minimizing Fees Charged by Investment Managers and Funds

Investment fees can substantially impact your long-term returns. Explore strategies to reduce these costs including:

- Low-Cost Index Funds: Consider investing in low-cost index funds or exchange-traded funds (ETFs) to reduce expense ratios.
- Utilizing Fee-Free Fixed and Fixed-Indexed Annuities in Retirement
- Minimizing the Use of Mutual Funds that have fees over .25% per year

Review and Consolidate Investments

Streamline your investment portfolio to minimize fees:

- Consolidate Accounts: Merge multiple accounts to avoid multiple sets of fees.
- Tax-Efficient Investing: Invest tax-efficiently to reduce capital gains taxes. If you can not do that effectively by yourself, please seek professional advice to do this.

Reducing Fees in Estate Transfers and Probate: Estate Planning to Minimize Probate

Probate can be costly and time-consuming. Explore ways to reduce these expenses:

- Revocable Living Trusts: Use trusts to avoid probate for certain assets, reducing legal fees and delays.
- Beneficiary Designations: Ensure that assets like life insurance policies and retirement accounts have clear beneficiary designations to bypass probate.

Estate Tax Planning

For larger estates, consider strategies to minimize estate taxes:

- Gift Tax Exclusion: Use the annual gift tax exclusion to transfer assets to heirs tax-free.
- Estate Tax Planning: Work with an estate planning attorney to implement tax-efficient strategies, such as credit shelter trusts.

Navigating Tax and Fee Reduction

Complex tax and fee reduction strategies often require professional advice:

- Tax Professionals: Consult with tax professionals, including CPAs and tax attorneys, for personalized tax planning.
- Estate Planning Attorneys: Work with estate planning attorneys to structure your estate efficiently.

Continual Monitoring and Adaptation

Tax laws and fees can change over time, so it's essential to stay informed and adapt your financial strategies accordingly.

Conclusion

Effectively reducing fees and taxes in your personal budget, investment portfolio, and estate transfers is a critical step in wealth building and preservation. By adopting tax-efficient spending habits, managing investment costs, and implementing strategic estate planning, you can retain more of your wealth, helping you achieve your financial goals and secure your legacy. In the next chapter, we will explore the importance of philanthropy and giving back to the community as part of your wealth-building journey.

CHAPTER 33

GEOGRAPHIC ARBITRAGE

You can leverage opportunities to move around the globe, or to move to other states.

In an increasingly interconnected world, geographic leverage has become a powerful strategy for building and preserving wealth. Geographic leverage involves making and saving money in one country with a strong economy and currency, then relocating to another country with a lower cost of living or favorable currency exchange rates. This approach can significantly enhance one's quality of life and stretch retirement savings or investment returns further.

For Black individuals and families looking to maximize their financial potential, geographic leverage presents a unique opportunity to overcome economic challenges and achieve financial independence.

The Concept of Geographic Leverage

Geographic leverage takes advantage of economic disparities between countries. By earning in a high-income country and spending in a lower-cost country, individuals can enjoy a higher standard of living than they might be able to afford at home. This strategy is especially relevant in retirement planning but can also be applied to digital nomads, remote workers, and entrepreneurs.

Key Benefits:

1. Cost Savings: Lower living costs mean your money goes further, covering expenses such as housing, food, healthcare, and entertainment at a fraction of the cost.
2. Enhanced Lifestyle: Lower costs can afford a higher quality of life, including access to better housing, dining, and leisure activities.
3. Tax Advantages: Some countries offer favorable tax regimes for expatriates, which can further enhance savings.

4. Cultural Enrichment: Living in a different country can provide rich cultural experiences and broaden one's perspective.

Making Money in the United States and Leveraging This Income in Other Countries

The United States is an ideal place to earn and save money. High-paying jobs, especially in fields such as technology, finance, healthcare, and engineering, provide ample opportunities to build substantial savings. Moreover, the U.S. offers a range of investment options, from real estate to stock markets, which can help grow wealth.

Steps to Build Wealth in the U.S.:

1. Maximize Income: Focus on career growth, side hustles, or entrepreneurial ventures to increase earnings.
2. Reduce Debt: Pay off high-interest debt to free up more money for savings and investments.
3. Invest Wisely: Diversify investments to include stocks, real estate, fixed or fixed indexed annuities, retirement accounts, or whatever else your preference is.
4. Save Aggressively: Take advantage of tax-advantaged accounts like 401(k)s, IRAs, and HSAs to build a financial cushion.

Geographic Leverage: Relocating to a Cheaper (or more attractive) State or Country

South America, for example, offers several countries with lower costs of living and favorable exchange rates for those earning or holding savings in U.S. dollars. Countries like Colombia, Ecuador, and Argentina are popular destinations for expatriates seeking to leverage their wealth.

Example: Moving to Colombia:

- Cost of Living: Colombia has a significantly lower cost of living compared to the U.S. For example, rent in a major city like Medellín can be as much as 70% cheaper than in cities like New York or San Francisco.

• Healthcare: Colombia offers high-quality healthcare at a fraction of the cost of the U.S. The country's healthcare system is highly ranked, providing excellent medical services at affordable prices.

• Lifestyle: With its warm climate, vibrant culture, and diverse landscapes, Colombia offers a rich and fulfilling lifestyle. Cities like Medellín and Bogotá are modern, cosmopolitan hubs with plenty of amenities and activities.

Financial Impact:

• Housing: Renting a modern apartment in a desirable area of Medellín might cost around $500-$800 per month, compared to $3,000 or more in a similar U.S. city.

• Utilities and Groceries: Utility bills and groceries are also significantly cheaper, allowing for substantial monthly savings.

• Healthcare: Private health insurance in Colombia can cost as little as $50-$100 per month, providing high-quality coverage.

Practical Considerations

1. Residency and Visas: Research the visa and residency requirements for your chosen country. Many countries offer retirement visas or digital nomad visas that allow long-term stays.

2. Language and Culture: Learning the local language and understanding cultural nuances can enhance your experience and integration into the community.

3. Financial Management: Maintain a bank account in both countries to manage your finances effectively. Consider the impact of currency exchange rates and fees.

4. Legal and Tax Implications: Understand the tax obligations in both the U.S. and your new country. Seek advice from a tax professional to navigate international tax laws and maximize benefits.

5. Take care of any life insurance, disability insurance, and other coverages you may want to get beforehand if you are going outside of the country.

Conclusion

Geographic leverage is a compelling strategy for building and preserving Black wealth. It's also a compelling strategy for being able to enjoy other cultures, eat great food, have access to healthier food and lifestyles, and for having lots of fun. By making and saving money in a strong economy like the United States and relocating to a country with lower living costs, individuals can significantly enhance their financial well-being and quality of life. Countries like Panama, Portugal, Costa Rica, and even Japan, depending on the situation, can provide excellent options for those looking to leverage their wealth globally. As with any financial strategy, thorough research and planning are essential to ensure a smooth transition and optimal benefits.

CHAPTER 34

THE HOLY GRAIL: PASSIVE INCOME

"If you don't find a way to make money while you sleep, you will work until you die." – Warren Buffett

In the quest to achieve financial freedom, passive income emerges as the cornerstone for building sustainable wealth. Unlike active income, where your time is directly exchanged for money, passive income allows you to earn while you sleep.

Many millionaires have multiple streams of income and DO NOT have all of their money sitting in just stocks, bonds, and mutual funds. Many of them also have multiple streams of passive income.

So what is the former bank CEO that handled clients with tens of millions to billions of dollars doing with his portfolio? For the past 5 years he's been working to transform his assets into passive income and guaranteed income streams.

This chapter explores diverse strategies to establish passive income streams, providing actionable insights for readers to secure their financial future.

Dividend Stock Investing

Dividend stocks are one of the most straightforward ways to generate passive income. By investing in companies with a strong track record of paying dividends, you receive regular payouts, typically quarterly. Dividend Aristocrats—companies with a history of increasing dividends for 25 years or more—are a good starting point for stable, predictable income. Reinvesting dividends can amplify your wealth through the power of compounding.

Real Estate Investment Trusts (REITs)

REITs are an excellent way to invest in real estate without the responsibilities of property management. By purchasing shares in REITs, you gain exposure to commercial real estate, including offices, malls, and apartment buildings, while earning dividends derived from rental income and property sales.

Short-Term Rentals (Airbnb and VRBO)

Platforms like Airbnb and VRBO have revolutionized real estate investing. By owning or managing short-term rental properties, you can generate substantial income, particularly in tourist-heavy areas. Effective property management and pricing strategies are critical for maximizing occupancy and returns.

Private Credit Lending

Private credit lending involves providing loans to businesses or individuals in exchange for interest payments. These loans often have higher yields than traditional fixed-income investments, though they come with increased risk. These are not recommendations and you must do your own due diligence, but platforms like PeerStreet or LendingClub facilitate access to private lending opportunities.

Litigation Credit Funding

Litigation funding involves providing financial support to plaintiffs in legal cases in exchange for a portion of the settlement. This high-risk, high-reward strategy requires careful due diligence but can yield significant returns.

Hard Money Real Estate Lending

Hard money loans are short-term, asset-backed loans used primarily in real estate transactions. By acting as a lender, you earn interest income, often at rates higher than traditional mortgages. These loans typically cater to real estate investors needing quick capital for property acquisitions or renovations.

Structured Notes

Structured notes are investment products that combine bonds with derivatives to offer customized returns. They can be an excellent tool for generating high passive income, often yielding up to 15% annually.

However, it's crucial to understand the underlying assets and terms before investing.

Real Estate Rental Income

Owning rental properties, including single-family homes and multifamily units, remains a cornerstone of passive income. Multifamily properties, in particular, offer economies of scale and higher income potential. Proper property management ensures consistent cash flow and mitigates vacancies.

Tax Lien Investing

Purchasing tax liens involves buying the unpaid property taxes of homeowners. In return, you receive interest payments or acquire the property at a significant discount if the homeowner defaults. Research local laws and auction procedures to succeed in this niche.

Affiliate Link Sales

Affiliate marketing allows you to earn a commission by promoting other companies' products or services. By leveraging platforms like Amazon Associates or ShareASale, you can create a steady stream of passive income through your blog, website, or social media. One example of an affiliate link opportunity is the opportunity to help spread the message of this book through our affiliate link tab that can be found at https://buildblkwealth.com/affiliate-program/.

Stock Trading

While stock trading is typically considered active income, strategies like covered call writing or selling put options can generate passive income from existing stock holdings. Automated trading platforms can also simplify this process.

Cryptocurrency Trading

The cryptocurrency market offers opportunities for passive income through staking, lending, and yield farming. Platforms like Coinbase allow investors to earn interest on their holdings while participating in decentralized finance (DeFi) ecosystems

Passive Income Business Models

Building businesses that generate passive income is an ultimate goal. Examples include:

- E-commerce Stores: Automate through drop-shipping or by hiring fulfillment services.
- Content Creation: Earn from ad revenue, subscriptions, or licensing for videos, blogs, or podcasts.
- Digital Products: Create and sell eBooks, courses, or templates.
- Franchise Ownership: Gain a share of profits while franchisees manage operations.

By diversifying across these strategies, you create multiple income streams that reduce dependence on a single source and build long-term financial stability. Passive income is not merely a financial tool—it is a pathway to freedom, providing the means to focus on what truly matters: family, health, and personal fulfillment.

Resources

We practice what we preach, so we aren't going to reinvent the wheel when it comes to providing you with more actionable ideas on how to generate passive income. Instead, we will refer you to already curated resources and experts like some of the ones below that we have listened to and learned from over the years.

Here's a curated list of excellent podcasts, YouTube channels, and websites if you are interested in developing passive income streams:

Podcasts

1. **Smart Passive Income with Pat Flynn**

Pat Flynn provides actionable advice and inspiring interviews to help entrepreneurs build income streams, automate processes, and achieve financial freedom.

2. **Cashflow Ninja with M.C. Laubscher**

This podcast dives deep into strategies for creating cash flow through real estate, business, and alternative investments.

3. **The One Percent with Ryan Daniel Moran**

Focused on creating wealth and building impactful businesses, this podcast explores practical steps to earn passive income.

4. **BiggerPockets Real Estate Podcast**

A must-listen for real estate investors, this podcast covers strategies for generating passive income through rental properties, house hacking, and REITs.

5. **The Side Hustle Show**

Hosted by Nick Loper, this podcast is packed with ideas and success stories for turning side hustles into sustainable passive income streams.

<u>YouTube Channels</u>

1. **Ryan Scribner**

Focused on personal finance and investing, Ryan offers insights into building wealth through dividend stocks, real estate, and online businesses.

2. **Graham Stephan**

Graham shares strategies for financial independence, including rental property investing and passive income tips.

3. **Andrei Jikh**

A finance and investing channel covering topics like cryptocurrency, stock market strategies, and passive income tools.

<u>Websites</u>

1. **Passive Income MD**

Aimed at professionals looking to create multiple income streams, this site covers real estate investing, REITs, and other passive income opportunities.

2. **Side Hustle Nation**

A comprehensive resource featuring ideas, guides, and case studies for starting and scaling passive income ventures.

These resources offer a wealth of knowledge to inspire and guide you toward creating sustainable passive income streams.

If you're even slightly thinking about generating passive income, take action today. Your journey toward a lifetime of substantial passive income (or even enough to let you make work optional) can begin with a single step.

Disclaimer: Just like everything else in this book, none of this is a recommendation or promotion. This is simply publicly available information, organized for you here, so that you can dig in and do more due diligence and research on your own, or speak with an expert about your particular age, knowledge level, wealth level, and situation.

CHAPTER 35

HEALTH = WEALTH

Disclaimer:

As always, and as with everything else in this book, everyone is different, so you need to do your own research, consult with your own physicians or other healthcare experts, and make your own decisions.

While the pursuit of financial prosperity is a significant aspect of building Black wealth and creating opportunities for happiness, it should never come at the expense of your health. In this chapter, we'll explore the connection between health and wealth, emphasizing why maintaining good health is an integral part of the wealth-building journey.

Understanding the Wealth of Health

It's easy to overlook the role that health plays in wealth. Health isn't just about the absence of illness; it's a state of physical, mental, and emotional well-being. Here's why it forms the bedrock of wealth:

- Productivity: Good health enhances your productivity, allowing you to work efficiently and achieve more in less time.
- Reduced Medical Costs: Preventive healthcare reduces the financial burden of medical expenses.
- Mental Clarity: Mental health contributes to decision-making and problem-solving, crucial for financial success.
- Longevity: A healthy lifestyle can lead to a longer life, giving you more time to enjoy the fruits of your labor.

The Cost of Poor Health: Medical Expenses and Lost Income

Health-related expenses, including doctor's visits, medications, and time away from work due to illness, can take a toll on your finances.

According to the Kaiser Family Foundation, Americans owe over $220 billion in medical debt as of 2024. And according to the CDC, 90% of the nation's $4.5 Trillion in annual health care expenditures are for people with chronic and mental health conditions.

Poor health can hinder your ability to build wealth in various ways:

- Reduced Income: Illness may lead to job loss, reduced work hours, or early retirement.
- High Medical Debt: Coping with medical bills can result in crippling debt.
- Lower Quality of Life: Poor health diminishes your overall life satisfaction, regardless of your financial status.

Strategies for Health and Wealth: The Holistic Approach

To embrace the idea that health equals wealth, adopt a holistic approach to your well-being:

- Healthy Diet: A balanced diet fuels your body and mind for peak performance.
- Regular Exercise: Physical activity not only enhances physical health but also reduces stress and boosts mental well-being.
- Drinking More Water
- Mental Health Care: Prioritize your mental health through practices like meditation, therapy, and stress management.
- Preventive Care: Regular check-ups and screenings can catch health issues early, preventing costly treatments later.
- Sleep: Good sleep can be as impactful as all the other things listed above in terms of keeping you healthy, productive, and happy.

Additionally, here are some other ideas that you can independently research on your own:

- Sauna
- Sun (getting more sun)
- Stress Reduction
- Massage
- Meditation
- Sound therapy

- Apple Cider Vinegar
- Turmeric
- Shakhti Mats
- Yoga
- Hot Yoga

Health as an Investment: Healthy Choices as Wealth-Building Tools

View your health-related decisions as investments in your future wealth by considering the following opportunities:

- Wellness Programs: Take advantage of workplace wellness programs and health incentives to reduce healthcare costs.
- Healthy Habits: Cultivate habits like adequate sleep, hydration, and stress reduction that contribute to both health and productivity.
- Preventive Health: Allocate a portion of your budget to preventive healthcare, such as annual check-ups and vaccinations.

Conclusion

Health and wealth are deeply intertwined, and the concept that "health equals wealth" is more than just a catchy phrase—it's a fundamental truth. Prioritizing your health is not a detour on the road to wealth; it's a critical part of the journey itself. By maintaining good health, you enhance your productivity, reduce financial stress, and ensure you have the energy and time to enjoy the wealth you've worked so hard to build. In the final chapter of this book, we'll reflect on the broader significance of building Black wealth and its role in transforming communities and creating lasting positive change.

CHAPTER 36

THE BIG PAYOFF

In the preceding chapters, we've discussed the fundamental steps and strategies needed to build Black wealth. Now, it's time to explore the profound transformation that unfolds when you take action and commit to these principles. Building Black wealth is not just a destination; it's a journey that can lead to personal and community transformation.

<u>Empowerment Through Knowledge</u>

When you invest time and effort in financial education and awareness:

1. Empowerment: You gain the knowledge and confidence to make informed financial decisions, and to increase your wealth in a methodical fashion.

2. Informed Choices: Armed with financial literacy, you can navigate the complex world of money management, and you can actually SIMPLIFY the process of building wealth. SIMPLIFICATION is KEY.

3. Resourcefulness: You learn how to seek out opportunities and adapt to financial challenges.

By participating in financial literacy programs and sharing your knowledge you gain:

<u>Financial Control and Growth</u>

Implementing budgeting and expense tracking in your life leads to:

1. Financial Discipline: You learn to manage your finances and make purposeful spending decisions.

2. **Savings Accumulation:** Budgeting helps you allocate resources efficiently, allowing for the growth of savings and investments.

<u>Stress Reduction and Mental Well-being</u>

When you have a handle on your finances:

1. Stress Reduction: Financial stability leads to reduced stress and anxiety, improving your overall quality of life.

2. Mental Clarity: Clarity about your financial situation enhances your mental well-being, aiding in better decision-making and the ability to focus on making more money, spending more free time with your family and friends, or accomplishing other goals that you may have.

Debt Freedom

Developing a debt repayment plan and exploring debt consolidation options leads to:

1. Financial Freedom: As you pay down high-interest debts, you free yourself from financial burdens and stress.

2. Wealth-Building Momentum: Eliminating debt allows you to redirect funds toward savings and investments, accelerating your wealth-building journey.

Financial Stability

Building savings and an emergency fund provides:

1. Peace of Mind: Knowing you have a financial safety net in place offers peace of mind, reducing financial anxiety.

2. Stability: In times of crisis or unexpected expenses, you're financially prepared, avoiding unnecessary setbacks and avoiding the crises that can put you in a hole you can't get out of.

Long-Term Prosperity

By consistently contributing to retirement accounts and TRULY diversifying your investments beyond just the 60-40 stock to bond split you can achieve:

1. Financial Security: You work toward a secure retirement, ensuring a comfortable and stress-free future with plenty of income in retirement.

2. Wealth Growth: Investments have the potential to be sustained, grow significantly over time, provide income for you in retirement, and still create generational wealth.

Conclusion

The journey to building Black wealth is transformative, both personally and communally. As you take action and embrace these principles of financial education, budgeting, debt reduction, savings, investment, and estate planning, you're not only securing your own future but also playing a pivotal role in uplifting your community and paving the way for lasting positive change. The journey is ongoing, and the rewards are boundless. It's time to embrace the transformational power of action and embark on the path to Black wealth.

CHAPTER 37

TAKING ACTION

What good is all of this information if you don't use it or ask someone to help you implement it?

Building BLK Wealth is not merely an aspiration; it's a journey that demands action. In this chapter, we'll explore the importance of taking proactive steps and provide guidance on the initial actions to embark upon the path to financial prosperity.

From Aspiration to Achievement

Many individuals harbor dreams of financial success, but it's action that transforms those dreams into reality. Taking action is the catalyst that propels you from where you are now to where you want to be.

Overcoming Inertia

Procrastination and indecision can hinder progress. By taking action, you break through the inertia that keeps you stagnant and set the wheels of progress in motion.

Key Action Steps to Start Building BLK Wealth

1. **Financial Education and Awareness**

Before diving into financial decisions, invest time in educating yourself about money matters:

- Read and Learn: Start with books, online resources, and reputable financial publications to gain knowledge about personal finance.
- Financial Literacy Programs: Seek out community resources and workshops focused on financial education.

At Ready2Retire we provide educational workshops on a weekly and monthly basis. We also provide workshops via the Foundation for Fiduciary Education in person around the country.

2. **Budgeting and Expense Tracking**

Understanding where your money goes is the foundation of financial control and growth:

- Create a Budget: Develop a realistic budget that accounts for your income, expenses, savings, and debt repayment.
- Expense Tracking: Monitor your spending diligently to identify areas where you can cut costs and save more.

There are plenty of budgeting apps and tools available to help you do this efficiently.

3. **Debt Reduction and Management**

We are not totally opposed to what Dave Ramsey teaches. In fact, his teachings on how to reduce debt, how to get moving in terms of investing, and how to look forward towards a better financial life are completely on point.

In terms of action, high-interest debt can be a significant roadblock to wealth-building:

- Debt Repayment Plan: Develop a strategy to pay down high-interest debts systematically.
- Debt Consolidation: Explore options for consolidating high-interest debts into lower-rate loans.

4. **Savings and Emergency Fund**

Building a financial safety net is crucial for stability and future investments:

- Emergency Fund: Establish an emergency fund that covers at least three to six months' worth of living expenses.
- Automate Savings: Set up automatic transfers to your savings or investment accounts.

5. **Investment and Retirement Planning**

Growing wealth requires strategic investment:

- Retirement Accounts: Contribute consistently to retirement accounts like 401(k)s and IRAs.

• Diversified Portfolio: Develop an investment strategy that aligns with your goals and risk tolerance.

6. **Estate Planning**

Ensure your financial legacy is preserved and passed on:

• Create a Will: Draft a clear and legally binding will that outlines asset distribution and guardianship for dependents.

• Trusts: Consider using trusts to protect assets and reduce estate taxes.

We recommend that you use an attorney to create these documents. The devil is in the details, and you want to make sure that you didn't save a few hundred dollars to cost you tens or hundreds of thousands down the line.

Cultivating a Mindset of Continuous Action

The journey to building Black wealth is ongoing. Commit to making continuous progress, even when faced with setbacks or challenges.

Seeking Support and Guidance

Surround yourself with mentors, advisors, and a community of individuals who share your financial aspirations. They can provide guidance, support, and accountability.

Conclusion

The road to building Black wealth begins with the crucial step of taking action. By starting with these initial action steps—educating yourself, budgeting, managing debt, saving, investing, and planning for your financial legacy—you set yourself on a trajectory of growth, security, and prosperity. Remember that building Black wealth is not a solitary endeavor; it's a collective journey that can uplift not only your life but also your community and future generations. In the final chapter of this book, we'll reflect on the broader significance of building Black wealth and its role in creating positive change on a larger scale.

CHAPTER 38

ADDITIONAL RESOURCES

Additional Podcasts

- The Cashflow Ninja (I recommend you scan through and listen to at least 10 podcasts)

Additional Reading:

- The Global Superstar™ by Benjamin Green - first 15 pages, at least one career chapter, and then last 3 chapters
- Getting to Yes by Roger Fisher & William Ury
- The Goal by Eliyahu M. Goldratt

Additional TV shows to watch

- Madoff documentary (on Netflix)
- MLK vs. FBI documentary (on Amazon)
- Teddy Pendergrass documentary (on Amazon)
- Rick James documentary (on Hulu)
- The Godfather I, II, and III

Additional Courses to Take & Workbooks to Complete

- Building Generational Wealth, Health, & Happiness Course Workbook
- The Cash Compound Silver plan (thecashcompound.com)

Additional Apps

- Calm (Daily Meditation App)
- Better Sleep

CHAPTER 39

THE CASE STUDIES

This chapter presents real-life case studies from our experience working with thousands of clients over the years. Names and locations have been omitted to protect privacy, but the lessons learned are invaluable for building and preserving wealth.

The Good

These stories highlight success through proper planning and execution of wealth building principles:

1. **The Mom Who Beat the Odds**

After a divorce in the South, this well-educated woman had no funds for a house down payment. She:

- Saved to buy a house.
- Established a 401(k) and a brokerage account for mutual funds.
- Transitioned into fixed indexed annuities, multi-year guaranteed annuities, and money market accounts.
- Maximized Social Security and her pension
- Acquired long-term care insurance
- Paid off her mortgage.
- Used required minimum distributions (RMDs) to fund whole life insurance, allowing her to leave over $300,000 tax-free to her heirs.

2. **The T Family**

A Georgia couple with $250,000 in annual guaranteed income (pensions and Social Security), no debt, and $3.5 million in pre-tax retirement accounts:

- Converted the majority of their retirement accounts to Roth IRAs, creating a $2.7 million tax-free bucket.

• Are implementing gifting strategies for their children and grandchildren with their pre-tax (401k) retirement accounts

• Expect to leave $5–$7.5+ million tax-free to their family due to compounding growth.

3. **A former CEO's Expertise Meets Reality**

A former private banker from Arizona worth $20 million who struggled to turn his assets into reliable retirement income. He realized how taxation, potential market volatility, and inflation could ruin retirement, so he has sought to protect his wealth while structuring it into sustainable income streams that include:

- Private credit funds
- Structured notes
- Real estate investment trusts
- Fixed indexed annuities
- Dividend stocks
- Charitable remainder unitrusts

The Bad

These cases highlight missed opportunities and challenges due to inadequate planning or external factors:

4. **DK's Fight for Financial Stability after the unexpected loss of a spouse**

A 61-year-old widow in Florida supporting two kids after her husband's death:

• Faces $300,000 in mortgage debt and $20,000 in student loans that remain to be paid after her husband's passing, since he only had a modest amount of life insurance (with our planning the husband would have had at least $500,000 in life insurance to cover the mortgage, student loan debt, and leave at least $100,000 to cover future expenses)

• Will need to work another seven years and follow a disciplined savings and investment plan that we have outlined to retire partially (will still have to work part time due to lack of funds passed on when husband passed away).

5. **K and John in Wisconsin**

A 65 and 71-year old couple with:

- Only 2 months worth of monthly expenses in the bank
- No Medicare supplemental plan
- No 401k, TSP, or IRA
- A sizable mortgage left to pay
- A sizable student loan left to pay
- The real prospect of having to work for the rest of their lives to make at least an additional $25,000 per year to meet their financial obligations.

6. **59-year old woman in Texas**

She was:

- Burning through her life savings and on track to run out of money in 4 years before meeting our team.
- On track to have her house foreclosed on in 4 years and become homeless without a financial plan

---

The Ugly

These stories illustrate the severe consequences of poor financial planning or lack of protection:

7. **A Young Family's Tragic, Permanent Loss**

A young man was diagnosed with cancer at 24, beat it, but then succumbed to brain cancer at 28.

- Left behind a wife, a 4-year-old, and a 1-year-old with no life insurance.
- His family was financially devastated.

8. **The Daughter and Mother's Retirement Sacrifice**

A mother's 37-year-old daughter, widowed with four kids, was left with only $40,000 in life insurance. The mother had to:

- Return to work to support her daughter's family.
- Postpone her retirement dreams indefinitely.

9. **The Charlotte Gal**

A 29-year-old earning $50,000 a year with three kids, driving a $70,000 car, and only $1,000 in savings. She aspires to retire by 45 but lacks a realistic plan and will likely never be able to fully retire.

10. **The Lady in Columbia, SC**

A 59-year old woman who is:

- renting her home but would like to purchase a house if she can
- is stuck in a job she hates for at least five more years due to financial obligations
- has no way to retire within 6 years without significant lifestyle changes.

11. **The former executive's Vulnerability**

A former executive from a publicly traded company has decided to roll the dice and not take out life insurance even though his wife is counting on his income for life and will lose it if he passes away. His wife is currently at risk of financial ruin upon his death, yet he chosen not to address this issue or Long-Term care.

12. **Uncooperative Spouses In General**

We've seen hundreds of cases over the years where one spouse refuses to look at reality and seek opportunities to fill potential gaps in family financial planning, leaving their families and children in precarious financial situations.

Key Lessons

- **Plan Early**: Waiting to address financial planning often leads to missed opportunities.
- Life Insurance Is Critical: Inadequate protection leaves families vulnerable.
- **Avoid Debt Traps**: Spending beyond one's means jeopardizes long-term goals.
- **Tax Efficiency Matters**: Strategies like Roth conversions and tax-free life insurance can maximize wealth transfer.
- **Income Is King**: Building predictable income streams is essential for a secure retirement.

This chapter underscores the power of preparation, but they also highlight the risks of misinformation and putting your head in the sand. We encourage you to learn from these stories to make informed decisions and secure your financial future.

CHAPTER 40

THE PRO ATHLETE FINANCIAL PLAYBOOK

The Summary:

Just like in other pro (and now college sports), one year you may be on top, and the next year you may be forgotten. The NFL stands for the National Football League. It also stands for "Not For Long". The average NFL career lasts for approximately 2.5 years, and over 60% of former NFL players face financial difficulty only 2 years after retirement. Basketball players, actors, actresses, rappers, and lots of other sports and entertainment professionals face the same financial challenges after they hang it up.

We hope you have a long, super successful career like Michael Jordan, Lebron James, Tom Brady, Denzel Washington, or Mariah Carey. That would be fantastic. But if you don't, you can still be financially successful if you follow the steps (and seek professional, reliable advice).

The Goal:

After you've gotten paid or gotten a deal done, the goal is to ultimately:

- Limit financial risks while growing wealth at least at the pace of annual inflation.
- Keep yourself wealthy and successful, even after the games or the gigs stop.
- Provide yourself with as much financial education/understanding as you desire.
- Look towards opportunities to create Generational Wealth and build Passive Income.

The Risks for NIL recipients, professional athletes, and entertainers:

- Family and entourage expenses
- A shorter than expected career

- Lawsuits
- Money-losing investments
- Not having your money keep pace with inflation
- Outliving your savings

The overall plan to overcome these risks:

Goals & Vision: Work to create a goal and vision for:

- The next year
- 3 years
- 10 years
- 20 years

Budget: The budget (or buckets) will include:

- The Fun Bucket
- Fixed Expenses Bucket (car notes, mortgages or rental expense, utilities, term life insurance (for family asset protection), etc.)
- Taxes Bucket
- Savings, Investment, & Generational Wealth Bucket

A sample budget for one of our clients that signs a $1 million contract might look like this:

- Fun: 20% ($200,000)
- Fixed Expenses: 20% ($200,000)
- Taxes: 30% ($300,000)
- SIGW: 30% ($300,000)

The Tax Plan:

The plan, in conjunction with an accountant, will include:

- Setting up LLCs to potentially run individual business and related expenses through
- Looking at options to be a resident of a no-income tax state
- Looking at real estate, oil/gas, and other investments that may help lower taxes
- Reviewing CRUTs (charitable remainder unitrusts) and other opps to lower taxes if appropriate

- Reviewing cash value whole life insurance as a tax-efficient storer of capital

Savings, Investment, & Generational Wealth Plan:

The plan will begin with a modeling of their future income based on their current contract plus current savings (via a LifeCycle model), and then looking at a product mix for their Generational Wealth Plan that includes:

- **Immediate/Emergency Needs Fund**: An immediate needs fund for emergencies, primary home purchases, and major planned expenses in next 12 months. It would sit in a high-yield savings account that the client owns (like CapitalOne).

- **Retirement plans**: Maximizing the leagues' retirement plans (NFL, NBA 401k)

- **Pensions**: Qualifying for and maximizing the pensions available

- **Index Funds**: Purchasing Low-cost, publicly traded funds based on principle that you can't beat market and hold these stocks/funds through large, well-known platforms like ETrade or Fidelity. Funds would include:
    - ▸Exchange Traded funds (The S&P 500 fund the SPY, The Nasdaq 100 fund the QQQ, The Russell 2000 Fund the IWM)
    - ▸Real estate investment trusts (REITs): Select, publicly traded REITs that pay dividends
    - ▸Master Limited Partnerships & Closed End Funds: Purchase select, publicly traded MLPs and CEFs that have low price-to-earnings ratios, are undervalued, and pay dividends aka the Taylor Swift strategy (https://canadianbusiness.com/ideas/what-does-taylor-swift-invest-in-discounted-closed-end-funds/)

• **S&P, Nasdaq, Dow Jones, Russell 2000, and large cap international stocks or ETFs**: The Stocks would be held via ETrade or Fidelity

• **Dividend stocks and funds**: Purchase well-known, publicly traded dividend paying stocks and ETFs (including the Dividend Aristocrats) to create passive income.

• **Multi-year Guaranteed Annuities**: Invest in A or A+ rated, 100+ year-old life insurance companies that are paying high guaranteed interest rates that you can lock for 3-10 years. These would have guaranteed principal, guaranteed interest rates, and no commissions or fees paid by the client. Depending on the amount, the amount would be spread across several companies not to exceed $500,000 per company.

• **Fixed Indexed Annuities**: Invest in A or A+ rated, 100+ year-old life insurance companies that have indexed funds like the S&P 500 that clients can attach funds to in order to have access to stock market upside without risking principal. These would have guaranteed principal, offer stock market upside, and have no commissions or fees paid by the client. Depending on the amount, the amount would be spread across several companies not to exceed $500,000 per company.

• **Managed Accounts**: You could elect to have a portion of their savings managed by a professional money manager. Fees would be limited to 1% per year, and based on volume of clients or the total amount under management, fees would be negotiated downwards. Money managers would be expected to try to control for volatility while seeking growth or income.

• **High-yielding CDs**: Up to 3 years, limited to $250,000 per bank or bank account.

• **Cash value Whole Life Insurance**: The plan serves as savings, a long-term care back up plan, a tax-free retirement plan (if withdrawn correctly), and as BYOB (be your own banker) option if they need to pull capital out for investment or purchase purposes. **Dabo Swinney (Clemson) and Jim Harbaugh (Michigan) have whole life insurance plans funded by schools (as comp) in place.**

- **Real estate**: You would review commercial and multifamily real estate opportunities.
- **Crypto, franchises, start ups, joint partnerships, and other business opportunities**: You could also review these opportunities from your "universe" along with other opportunities.

Note: Whole life insurance, Multiyear guaranteed annuities, and fixed indexed annuities are lawsuit and creditor-proof, and tax-advantaged.

From the total savings/investment/wealth bucket, an annual allocation for you could be:

- Immediate/Emergency Needs Fund in High-yielding checking: 10%
- Retirement plans: 5%
- Pensions: Whatever is allocated towards client Qualifying for and maximizing the pensions available
- Index Funds (plus REITS, MLPs, CEFs): 5%
- S&P, Nasdaq, Dow Jones, Russell 2000, and international stocks: 5%
- Dividend stocks and funds: 5%
- Multi-year Guaranteed Annuities: 10% (as long as interest rates remain historically high)
- Fixed Indexed Annuities (indexed to the S&P 500, Nasdaq): 20%
- Managed Accounts: 10%
- High-yielding CDs: 5%
- Cash value Whole Life Insurance: 10%
- Real estate: 5%
- Crypto, private equity, franchises, start-ups, joint partnerships: 10%

All of these potential allocations are of course subject to change.

Estate Plan:

You could be set up with (affordable) trusts, wills, and other legal directives drawn up with updated beneficiaries to ensure that plans were in place if something happened. This plan would go in conjunction with Tax Planning if we put charitable trusts, family foundations, or other legal vehicles in place to reduce their tax profile.

CHAPTER 41

ASSET ALLOCATIONS FOR DIFFERENT AGES

Disclaimer: As with the rest of this book, Please do your due diligence. Any investment decisions you make are your own.

Disclaimer for Ready2Retire LLC and R2R IP LLC

The information provided in this chapter is for informational purposes only and is not intended as financial, legal, or tax advice. While efforts have been made to ensure the accuracy of the information, Ready2Retire LLC and R2R IP LLC make no guarantees, warranties, or representations regarding the accuracy, reliability, or completeness of the content provided.

General Information

This material is intended to provide general information about financial topics and strategies and does not constitute personalized advice. Every individual's financial situation is unique, and specific advice tailored to your personal circumstances should be obtained from a qualified professional. You should consult with a licensed financial advisor, tax professional, or attorney before implementing any financial, tax, or legal strategies discussed herein.

No Guarantee of Results

Investments, including but not limited to those mentioned in this chapter, involve risks, including the potential loss of principal. Past performance is not indicative of future results. Asset allocation strategies, product selections, and planning approaches described herein are subject to changes in market conditions, individual circumstances, and applicable laws and regulations. There is no guarantee that the recommendations made will achieve your financial goals or that they will not result in losses.

No Fiduciary Relationship

Use of this material does not create a fiduciary relationship between you and Ready2Retire LLC, R2R IP LLC, or its representatives. Any reliance you place on the information contained in this chapter is strictly at your own risk.

Third-Party Products and Services

This material may mention financial products, services, or strategies offered by third parties. Ready2Retire LLC and R2R IP LLC do not endorse or guarantee any specific product, service, or provider and assume no responsibility for the performance, suitability, or reliability of third-party products or services.

Tax and Legal Implications

This material does not constitute tax or legal advice. Tax laws and regulations are subject to change, and their application can vary depending on individual circumstances. You are encouraged to consult with a licensed tax advisor or attorney to understand the implications of any financial decisions or strategies in the context of your personal situation.

Limitation of Liability

Ready2Retire LLC, R2R IP LLC, and their representatives shall not be held liable for any direct, indirect, incidental, or consequential damages resulting from the use or reliance on the information contained in this chapter. This includes, but is not limited to, loss of income, profits, or investments, even if advised of the possibility of such damages.

Ownership and Intellectual Property

This material is the intellectual property of Ready2Retire LLC and R2R IP LLC and is protected under copyright law. Unauthorized reproduction, distribution, or modification of this material, in whole or in part, is strictly prohibited without prior written consent.

By engaging with this material, you acknowledge and agree to the terms of this disclaimer. For additional information or clarification, please contact Ready2Retire LLC or R2R IP LLC directly.

Cracking the Code: The Portfolio of Products & Allocations for 2025 – 2035

The Basis for the idea:

- Volatility & Market Losses that can ruin portfolio (especially during the Retirement Red Zone years)
- Tens of thousands of articles, talks with financial advisors, aggregates of financial advisor reviews
- The paper "Beyond The Status Quo: A Critical Assessment of Lifecycle Investment Advice", published October 2, 2023 by Anarkulova, Cederburg, and O'Doherty
- The latest S&P 500 estimates from large investment firms for the next decade (2025 – 2035)

The Plan

1. 30% stocks including mix of:
    a. Dividend growers (individual stocks, ETFs, aristocrats)
    b. Russell 2000 ETF
    c. Small cap ETFs
    d. International ETF
    e. BlackRock Dynamic Allocation Index ETFs including heavier bond ETF weighting (BDYALVCX) (screenshot below)
    f. REITS
    g. MLPs
    h. Closed End Funds (discounted, Taylor Swift model)
    i. Commodity ETFs
2. 10% MYGAs from A or A+ rated carriers (depending on the interest rate)
3. 20% Structured notes (depending on the rates and risk)

4. 30% FIAs from A or A+ rated carriers (tracking indexes, Zebra models, Shiller, etc.)
5. 10% - Cash held in high-yielding (no lock-up) savings accounts

Why have you not heard of this from your financial advisor?

1. 70%+ of them are not insurance licensed, so they can't show you 70% of this solution. The only thing they can show you is variable annuities.
2. Many of them are listening to what their bosses say, which is to keep all assets in the market so they can make 1-2.5% in fees per year (regardless of the performance of your investments).

Why are you hearing it from me?

1. I run my own independent advisory (and business) with over 50 products (solutions), so I am not beholden to anyone.
2. I've lived in the future (Japan 8 years) so I have the benefit of forecasting from a different lens, verifying the accuracy of my past guesses, and then forecasting what happens if I'm 80% accurate again.
3. I've been through 1000 earthquakes, so after that, being controversial is no problem.
4. I have a financial-insurance-financial + retirement sandwich of experience. I have been on both sides and am super well-versed in both sides.
5. Because I've studied my ass off, listened to the smartest people from all sides of the aisle, and then come up with this solution that needs to be shared for this period (2025 – 2035).

CHAPTER 42

BLUEPRINT FOR WEALTH BUILDING & PRESERVATION

Building and preserving wealth requires a dynamic strategy that evolves with your age, goals, and risk tolerance. This chapter outlines optimal asset allocation and considerations for individuals at different life stages: 30, 50, 65, and 75 years old.

Disclaimer: We do not verify the accuracy of the chart below.

THE AVAILABLE TOOLS IN THE FINANCIAL FIDUCIARY TOOL BOX: THE DEFINITIVE COMPARISON

(partial list)	MYGAs	CDs	High-Yield Savings	IRAs	Stocks	Bonds	Stock & Bond Mutual Funds	Hybrid FIAs	
Tax-Deferred Growth	✓	✗	✗	✓	Yes, sometimes	Yes, sometimes	Yes, sometimes	✓	
Penalty-Free Withdrawal Options	✓	✗	✗	✓	✓	✓	✓	✓	
Guaranteed Fixed Interest Rates	✓	✓	✗	N/A	✗	✗	✗	✓	*for 1-yr at a time
Principal Protection	✓	✓	✓	✗	✗	✗	✗	✓	
FDIC-Insured	✗	✓	✓	✗	✗	✗	✗	✗	
Highly Regulated at National & State Level	✓	✓	✓	✓	✓	✓	✓	✓	
3 - 10 Year Options	✓	✗	✗	N/A	N/A	✓	N/A	✓	
Fee & Commission-Free Options	✓	✓	✓	✗	✓	✓	✗	✓	
				*Penalty-free post 59.5		*I Bonds are fee-free			

Asset Allocation for a 30 Year Old

Key Goals: Growth, risk-taking, and foundation building.
At this stage, your focus should be on aggressive growth strategies while laying the groundwork for long-term wealth preservation.

Asset Allocation Strategy:

- **Life Insurance**: 10x salary in a mix of term and whole life insurance for income replacement and wealth-building.
- **Emergency Savings**: Maintain six months' worth of living expenses in a high-yield savings or money market account.
- **Equity Investments**:

▸Brokerage accounts with dividend-paying, growth, and international stocks.

▸Real Estate Investment Trusts (REITs) for diversification.

- **Retirement Accounts**:

▸Maximize employer-sponsored IRA or 401(k) contributions with company match.

▸Open a Roth IRA for tax-free growth.

- **Alternative Investments**:

▸Crypto allocations can be up to 25% of your portfolio, emphasizing high-risk, high-reward potential.

- **Income-Producing Assets**: Consider rental properties or dividend-paying stocks.
- **Estate Planning**: Establish basic trusts and wills for future legacy.
- **Health**: Build healthy habits now to maximize future Social Security benefits.

Asset Allocation for a 50 Year Old

Key Goals: Preservation, moderate growth, and risk management. With retirement on the horizon, the focus shifts to balancing growth and stability.

Asset Allocation Strategy:

- **Life Insurance**: Increase coverage to 15x salary in a combination of term and whole life insurance.
- **Emergency Savings**: Build a 12-month emergency fund to safeguard against unforeseen events.
- **Fixed Income**:

▸Introduce Fixed Indexed Annuities (FIAs) for protection and steady growth.

- **Equity Investments**:

▸Maintain brokerage accounts with dividend-paying stocks, growth stocks, and REITs.

- **Retirement Accounts**:

▸Continue maximizing contributions to employer-sponsored IRAs and Roth IRAs.

- **Alternative Investments**:
  ▸Crypto allocation should not exceed 20% of total assets.
- **Income-Producing Assets**: Diversify income streams with real estate, permanent life insurance, and dividend-paying stocks.
- **Estate Planning**: Ensure trusts and wills are updated for tax efficiency and legacy goals.
- **Health**: Stay active and healthy to optimize long-term financial outcomes, including delayed Social Security benefits

---

Asset Allocation for a 65 Year Old (Debt-Free)

Key Goals: Stability, income generation, and risk reduction.
As retirement begins, protecting your nest egg while generating sustainable income becomes critical.

Asset Allocation Strategy:

- **Life Insurance**: Reduce to 5x salary or maintain a minimum of $250,000 coverage through term and whole life insurance.
- **Emergency Savings**: Keep 12 months of living expenses liquid.
- **Fixed Income**:
  ▸Use Fixed Indexed Annuities (FIAs) and Multi-Year Guaranteed Annuities (MYGAs) for reliable income and protection.
  ▸Incorporate structured notes for additional income with downside protection.
- **Equity Investments**:
  ▸Retain dividend-paying and growth stocks, international equities, and REITs for moderate growth.
- **Retirement Accounts**:
  ▸Strategically withdraw from Roth IRAs and other retirement accounts to minimize taxes.

- **Alternative Investments**:
    - ‣Crypto exposure should be reduced to no more than 15%.
- **Income-Producing Assets**: Continue leveraging real estate and permanent life insurance for tax-advantaged income.
- **Social Security**: Consider deferring benefits to maximize payouts, depending on health and financial need.
- **Estate Planning**: Finalize trusts, wills, and healthcare directives.

Asset Allocation for a 75 Year Old (Debt-Free)

Key Goals: Income sustainability, legacy planning, and wealth transfer. The focus shifts to income generation, reducing exposure to market volatility, and ensuring a smooth transfer of wealth.

Asset Allocation Strategy:

- **Life Insurance**: Maintain 5x salary or $250,000 minimum coverage through term and whole life insurance.
- **Emergency Savings**: Retain a 12-month emergency fund for immediate needs.
- **Fixed Income**:
    - ‣Rely more heavily on Fixed Indexed Annuities (FIAs), MYGAs, and structured notes for steady income.
- **Equity Investments**:
    - ‣Keep a smaller allocation in dividend-paying stocks, REITs, and international equities to outpace inflation.
- **Retirement Accounts**:
    - Prioritize tax-advantaged withdrawals from Roth IRAs.
- **Alternative Investments**:
    - ‣Crypto exposure should be limited to no more than 10%.
- **Income-Producing Assets**: Continue leveraging rental income and permanent life insurance benefits.
- **Social Security and Pensions**: Ensure these are fully optimized and serving as reliable income sources.

- **Estate Planning**: Regularly update estate documents to reflect changes in assets, beneficiaries, or tax laws.

Final Thoughts

Asset allocation evolves with age, but core principles remain constant: diversification, risk management, and aligning investments with life goals. By following these tailored strategies, individuals can build a robust financial plan that ensures growth, stability, and a lasting legacy.

CHAPTER 43

THE RETIREMENT INCOME PLAN

In retirement, a steady income isn't just about covering basic needs—it's about sustaining a lifestyle, ensuring peace of mind, and enjoying the fruits of your labor. Retirement income planning bridges the gap between what you've saved and how you use it effectively. Here's how the Ready2Retire™ Process (R2R), inspired by our wealth-building philosophy, helps you achieve both financial security and flexibility.

Step 1: Covering Your Basic Needs

The cornerstone of any retirement plan is ensuring that your essential needs are met. These include housing, food, healthcare, transportation, and inflation-adjusted discretionary spending.

- **Income Needs**: Determine your monthly income requirement based on current expenses, lifestyle goals, and expected inflation.
- **Turning Assets into Income**: The Requirements… After taking into account your guaranteed income streams, you may need to set aside between 25% to 70% of your portfolio for the purpose of generating income. We have sat in serious conversations with people worth $20 million who were concerned about generating enough income in retirement. You can never focus too much on income.
- **Solution**: Build a guaranteed income stream using tools like Social Security, pensions, fixed annuities, or dividends. These income streams ensure your essential expenses are consistently covered.

Key Takeaway: Financial independence begins with securing predictable, inflation-adjusted income for life.

Step 2: Establishing an Emergency Fund

Life is unpredictable, and even the best-laid plans require a safety net. This is where an emergency fund becomes essential.

- "Life Happens + Fun" Bucket: Allocate funds for unexpected expenses, such as a sudden health crisis, home repairs, or family emergencies. Also set funds aside for your vacations and having fun.
- Recommended Minimum: Keep at least $50,000—or 10% of your portfolio—liquid for immediate access.

Why It Matters: An emergency fund prevents you from dipping into long-term savings, which could derail your retirement strategy.

Step 3: Planning for Long-Term Healthcare Costs

As life expectancy increases, so do healthcare expenses. Proper planning can help you avoid financial strain in the later stages of retirement.

- **Allocation**: Reserve 20%–25% of your portfolio to cover long-term care, whether at home or in a nursing facility.
- **Considerations**: Costs for extended care can escalate significantly. Insurance products, such as long-term care policies, can help mitigate these risks.

Pro Tip: Address healthcare costs early to reduce uncertainty about future expenses.

Step 4: Growth-Oriented Investments

After securing basic needs and building a safety net, you can allocate the remaining funds toward higher-risk, growth-focused investments.

- **Asset Allocation**: Balance safe instruments (fixed indexed annuities, money market accounts) with riskier options (stocks, ETFs, real estate).
- **Portfolio Diversification**: A mix of taxable and tax-advantaged accounts ensures optimal growth while minimizing taxes.

Important Principle: The true value of a portfolio lies in the sustainable income it can generate, not just the total assets it holds.

The R2R Process in Practice

1. **Retirement Budgeting**

Assess your financial gaps between guaranteed income and monthly expenses. Fill those gaps using tailored solutions.

2. **Balancing Product Mix and Timing**

Choose financial tools that match your risk tolerance and time horizon:

- **Safe Investments**: Certificates of deposit, fixed indexed annuities, immediate guaranteed income annuities, savings bonds, and money market accounts.
- **Semi-safe Investments**: Structured notes, Buffered ETFs.
- **Riskier Investments:** Stocks, mutual funds, commodities, REITs (real estate investment trusts), and cryptocurrencies for long-term growth potential.

3. **Tax Efficiency**

Use a mix of taxable and non-taxable investment accounts to minimize tax burdens in retirement. Consider Roth conversions or life insurance solutions to leave a tax-free legacy. Also consult with someone to consider an appropriate and timely:

- Social Security claiming strategy

- RMD withdrawal strategy

Balancing Needs and Flexibility

As we emphasize, a successful retirement plan is about balancing financial goals with the right tools. Do you care what the tool is called or how it looks, as long as you get the job done? We hope not.

Be steadfast in your objectives but flexible in the methods you use to achieve them.

Closing Thoughts: Income is King

A secure retirement is not about the size of your portfolio but about the consistency of income it generates.

The Ready2Retire Process ensures:

- Basic needs are covered.
- Emergencies are manageable.
- The Fun times are also "Funded".
- Long-term risks are addressed.
- Growth opportunities align with your goals.

By following these principles, you can enjoy your retirement years while preserving wealth for future generations.

For more information, visit **Ready2Retire.net** or contact our team at **office@ready2retire.net**

Good luck. And make it happen. You have the intellect. You have the tools. And you have the power to make it happen.

ABOUT THE AUTHOR

As you can see, Ben Green has been around the world and back, a couple dozen times. A native of Columbia, SC, Ben is the Co-Founder of Ready2Retire™, a firm that is on track to become the leading retirement income planning and wealth preservation firm in the US. Ben has a great appreciation for customer service and client satisfaction honed from more than 20 years of experience, and is recognized nationwide as a top retirement, insurance, Medicare, and Social Security planner.

Ben is also President & COO of Insurance Advantage, an employee benefits agency he co-founded 13 years ago. He has over 3,000 clients, and including his volunteer work with the Foundation for Financial Education where he has provided financial counseling for staff at the CIA, Pentagon, Dept. of Treasury, The Tennessee Titans, The Washington Commanders, and dozens of other agencies and companies, he has provided financial literacy and counseling to over 10,000 people.

Ben has previously served as COO of a human resources staffing firm, and as Vice President of Asia & Europe for an American software company.

Ben has extensive experience in economic development and consulting, and worked as a Business Recruiter for South Carolina. Since Ben opened the Japan office in 2012, South Carolina has received over $2.2 billion in investment. In 2014, he was hired to write the Strategic Plan for the (entire) State of South Carolina, and has advocated for high-speed rail lines to be added to the transportation mix in South Carolina and the rest of the Southeast for the last 5 years.

Based on 10 years working overseas in Japan, Brazil, & Spain, he wrote the Amazon Best Seller The Global Superstar: How Your Students Can Develop an Advantage over Global Competition to help students prepare for careers in this changing economy.

He holds a Bachelor's degree in Finance from Morehouse College, an International MBA from The University of South Carolina, and certificates from UNC and Temple University. He's conversant in Japanese, Portuguese, & Spanish, and has served on numerous boards including the South Carolina Independent Colleges & Universities association, the SC Chamber of Commerce, and the Columbia (SC) Chamber of Commerce. He's a member of the Nashville City Club & the Nashville Kiwanis Club.

Ben splits time between his homes in Nashville, TN and Columbia, SC with his wife and their two wonderful daughters. He loves traveling, spending time with friends, spending time with his family, and helping his clients win in retirement.

Certifications & Education:

✓B.A. in Finance, Morehouse College, 1997

✓International Banking & Finance Continuing Education Certificate, Temple University Japan, 1998

✓Certificate in Brazilian Business & Portuguese Language, University of Sao Paulo, 2002

✓International MBA, University of South Carolina, 2003

✓Certified Mutual Fund Specialist certificate, 2006 – Present

✓Economic Development Certificate, University of North Carolina, 2007

✓Affordable Care Act Health Insurance Certifications, 2012 - Present

✓Medicare Certifications, 2016 – Present

✓Long-Term Care Insurance Certifications, 2016 – Present

✓Fixed Annuity Certifications, 2019 – Present

✓Certified Financial Fiduciary® designation, 2023 – Present

States we are licensed in:

‣SC, NC, GA, TN, KY, VA, MD, DC, CT, NJ, TX, LA, MS, FL, IL, PA, CA, AZ, NM, WA

‣Wherever you are, we can help you out (once we get licensed in that state). Licensing usually takes less than 5 days.

www.ingramcontent.com/pod-product-compliance
Lightning Source LLC
LaVergne TN
LVHW090951250926
848814LV00062B/23
9798218603571